OSPREY COMBAT AIRCRAFT • 80

LOCKHEED SR-71 OPERATIONS IN EUROPE AND THE MIDDLE EAST

SERIES EDITOR: TONY HOLMES

OSPREY COMBAT AIRCRAFT • 80

LOCKHEED SR-71 OPERATIONS IN EUROPE AND THE MIDDLE EAST

PAUL F CRICKMORE

OSPREY
PUBLISHING

Front cover
On 19 May 1977, mission planning for the SR-71's first operational sortie from RAF Mildenhall became particularly interesting for the crew of the reconnaissance aircraft when they discovered that the Soviet military had issued a Notice To Airman (NOTAM) stating their intention to test-fire a missile up to an altitude of 100,000 ft. This in itself was not unusual, but the coordinates into which the missile was to be fired quickly focused the minds of the mission planning cell at Mildenhall – they just happened to precisely bracket the SR-71's intended point of ingress and egress to/from the Barents Sea!

Hasty conference calls were convened between the base and the United States, and despite reservations expressed by SR-71 designer Kelly Johnson, the mission went ahead on 20 May. The resulting sortie, coordinated with an RC-135V 'Rivet Joint' electronic intelligence aircraft, proved to be an outstanding success, with both platforms capturing the radio frequency signals associated with the Soviet SA-5 'Gammon' surface-to-air missile (SAM).

The SR-71A involved in this historic mission was 64-17958, and it is depicted here just as its crew, Majs Tom Alison (pilot) and J T Vida (Reconnaissance Systems Officer), exit the collection area without attracting the unwanted attention of a Soviet SAM and head back to Mildenhall. After the mission, Alison recalled, 'J T and I had spent 45 minutes in the "denied area" specified by the NOTAM – most of it at a speed that was a little in excess of Mach 3. It was just another day at the office!' (*Cover artwork by Gareth Hector, based on a model supplied by MilViz Inc.*)

For Flt Lt Adam Paul Crickmore

First published in Great Britain in 2009 by Osprey Publishing
Midland House, West Way, Botley, Oxford, OX2 0PH, UK
44-02 23rd St, Suite 219, Long Island City, NY 11101, USA
Email: info@ospreypublishing.com

© 2009 Osprey Publishing Limited

ISBN: 978 1 84603 418 3
PDF e-book ISBN: 978 1 84908 085 9

Edited by Tony Holmes
Page design by Tony Truscott
Cover Artwork by Gareth Hector
Aircraft Profiles by Chris Davey
Index by Michael Forder
Printed and bound in China through Bookbuilders

10 11 12 13 14   11 10 9 8 7 6 5 4 3 2

FOR A CATALOGUE OF ALL BOOKS PUBLISHED BY OSPREY MILITARY AND AVIATION PLEASE CONTACT:

Osprey Direct, c/o Random House Distribution Center,
400 Hahn Road, Westminster, MD 21157
Email: uscustomerservice@ospreypublishing.com

Osprey Direct, The Book Service Ltd, Distribution Centre,
Colchester Road, Frating Green, Colchester, Essex, CO7 7DW
Email: customerservice@ospreypublishing.com

www.ospreypublishing.com

CONTENTS

THE DEPLOYMENT THAT NEVER WAS

The Six Day War in early June 1967 had seen Arab armed forces humiliated by the Israelis. Six years on, President Anwar al-Sadat of Egypt had decided that another conflict with Israel was necessary both to re-establish his nation's claims on former Egyptian land east of the Suez Canal and to restore Arab pride in the region. President Hafez al-Assad of Syria had agreed with the Egyptians to mount a simultaneous attack on the Jewish state from the north, and at 1400 hrs on 6 October 1973 (Yom Kippur Day – the Jewish Day of Atonement), Egyptian and Syrian forces began the coordinated attack with an hour-long barrage from 2000 artillery pieces positioned along Israel's western border. Some 240 Egyptian aircraft also hit three Israeli airfields and other important targets in the Sinai.

The aggressors were soon advancing along a 130-mile front, employing five infantry divisions that were in turn supported by three mechanised and two armoured divisions. As Israeli soldiers prayed in their bunkers in celebration of Yom Kippur, the Egyptian war machine rumbled over ten pontoon bridges that had been thrown across the Suez Canal, stormed the supposedly impregnable 'Bar-Lev Line' and established bridge-heads on the East Bank. To the north, the Syrian phase of the attack opened with another massive 30-minute artillery bombardment. This barrage preaged the advance of three infantry divisions and two armoured divisions, and was timed to coincide with an independent attack, mounted by Syrian helicopter-borne commandos, on the vital Israeli observation post at Mount Hermon, in the Golan Heights.

Poor intelligence, together with the speed and ferocity of the Arab attack, caught the Israelis off guard. Troops were mobilised from synagogues and radio stations broke their traditional silence during Yom Kippur to broadcast instructions to the threatened population. Most Western intelligence agencies were also surprised by the joint attack. However, three days prior to the onslaught, the Soviets had launched the camera-equipped satellite cosmos 596 from Plesetsk, in southwestern USSR, which allowed them to watch the battle on behalf of their Arab allies.

The Israelis regrouped within two days and attacked the pontoon bridges over the Suez Canal. In the north, however, the Syrians continued their push toward the River Jordan

SR-71A 64-17955 was used extensively by Air Force Systems Command (AFSC) and Lockheed for test and development programmes throughout the aircraft's frontline career. It was operating from Griffiss AFB on A-2 DEF evaluation flights, code named *Black Knight*, when the 9th SRW was tasked with overflying the Yom Kippur War battlefronts in October 1973. The wing used the AFSC operation as cover for its secret flights over the Middle East. Lockheed 'tech reps' and USAF personnel supporting 64-17955 were also called on by the 9th SRW when it came time to prepare its two frontline aircraft for *Giant Reach/Busy Pilot* missions. Note the famous Lockheed 'Skunk Works' motif on the tail of 64-17955 (*Lockheed*)

and the Sea of Galilee. The Soviet reconnaissance effort was strengthened on 8 October when Cosmos 597 was launched, this new satellite being more versatile than Cosmos 596 thanks to its ability to change orbits using rockets. Despite the resultant increase in the satellite's speed because of the weight associated with the rockets, the perigee improved photographic resolution. With its path now inclined 65° to the Equator, Cosmos 597 was aligned across both battlefronts.

On 9 October Cosmos 596 was recovered after returning to earth. By then, however, the ground situation had turned in favour of the Israelis. Syrian efforts in the north had ground to a halt after a furious battle, and Gen Ariel Sharon's forces in the south had successfully attacked the Egyptians and retaken a second-line fortification that had fallen the day before.

Cosmos 598 was launched on 10 October to improve surveillance of the war zone. Pitched slightly higher than the preceding Cosmos satellites, it was already in orbit when 597 returned its film cassettes to earth. The Soviets were also receiving real-time imagery from 598 via the Yevpatoriya tracking station in the Crimea.

Record breakers Lt Cols Tom Estes and Dewain Vick receive the 1972 Harmon International Trophy from Senator Barry Goldwater and President Richard Nixon (*USAF*)

As with all frontline SR-71 missions, the 9th SRW's dedicated KC-135Q fleet played a pivotal role in the *Giant Reach/Busy Pilot* operation (*via Paul F Crickmore*)

In response to the Soviet reconnaissance effort, the US government decided to step up its intelligence gathering operation. Having proven its worth in Vietnam, the Lockheed SR-71A of the 9th Strategic Reconnaissance Wing (SRW) offered the best quick reaction, hot-spot reconnaissance capability. Plans were duly drafted to fly missions from the aircraft's home at Beale AFB, in California, to Egypt, after which the jet would recover at RAF Mildenhall, in Suffolk. This long-range concept had been validated two years before when Lt Cols Tom Estes and Dewain Vick completed a gruelling 15,000-mile proving flight.

Commander in Chief Strategic Air Command (CINCSAC, pronounced 'sink-sac'), Gen John Meyer, ordered the CO of the 9th SRW, Col Pat Halloran, to prepare for these missions. The latter immediately realised that his unit's performance when carrying out this tasking would attract wide-ranging attention from within both US military and government circles.

SR-71 pilot and CO of the 9th SRW,
Col Pat Halloran headed the wing's
detachment at Griffiss AFB
(*Tom Pugh*)

The 9th SRW despatched SR-71As
64-17979 and 64-17964 to Griffiss
AFB to conduct *Giant Reach/Busy
Pilot* flights. They are seen here
together within a hangar at the
New York base, with the tail of
T-38 'Toxon 01' just in shot to the
right. The latter served as 64-
17955's chase aeroplane during
the *Black Night* A-2 DEF trials
(*Tom Pugh*)

Indeed, Halloran felt that the future of his wing, and the entire *Senior Crown* programme (the SR-71 programme's classified USAF codename), hinged on the successful execution of this mission.

Due to its importance, Halloran asked the new Fifteenth Air Force commander, Lt Gen Bill Pitts, for permission to 'run the show' himself. Having received the approval of the latter, Halloran put together a maintenance recovery team and headed to Mildenhall from Beale on a tanker. He would later recall;

'I was scheduled to go straight to London to brief senior Ministry of Defence (MoD) officials on the plan, but upon my arrival at Mildenhall I was informed that the British government had had second thoughts and was denying us authority to operate from the UK. I was then told that Griffiss AFB, in New York state, would be our operating location. Without rest, we turned the tanker around and the full complement of planners and maintenance personnel were reloaded for a quick return trip to the US. Undoubtedly, that was the shortest overseas TDY (temporary duty) in the history of the 9th SRW!'

It later became clear that the Conservative government, under Prime Minister Edward Heath, had denied the USAF the use of Mildenhall as a sop to the Arabs in the belief that this would guarantee continued oil supplies to the UK. This move singularly failed, however, and later produced heated exchanges between Europe and the US government.

Fortunately for the 9th SRW, Lockheed's Palmdale-based flight test SR-71A 64-17955 had already been scheduled to conduct evaluation flights with its new A-2 Defensive Electronic Systems (DEF) from Griffiss AFB from mid-October onwards. By stationing Beale's detachment there at the same time, Halloran could draw on additional support from Lockheed's technical field support personnel and have a convenient cover story for their secret operations into the Middle East.

As the 9th SRW's new operating location was firmed up, and higher headquarters approved the overall transatlantic plan, crews began serious flight planning for the first mission. Lt Col Jim Shelton and Maj Gary Coleman got airborne from Beale in 64-17979 at 2200 hrs on 11 October and headed for Griffiss. They were met by an angry base commander and three Lockheed tech reps after laying 'a heavy late-night sonic boom track' across the US and down into New York state as they made their descent from altitude. A phone call from Lt Col Shelton to Majs Al Joersz and John Fuller (who would fly a second SR-71

into Griffiss) advised them to make their descent profile over the Great Lakes so as to minimise the effects of the boom on the urban eastern states. Fortunately, there were no boom complaints when the second crew made their crossing. The next day's newspapers reported a strange phenomenon that was described by one scientist as a probable 'meteoric shock wave'.

The second aircraft, 64-17964, developed a hydraulic problem in flight that forced an engine-change upon its arrival at Griffiss, thus leaving the new detachment down to one mission-ready aeroplane until specialised equipment could be flown in from Beale. An hour after 64-17964 had landed, the first tanker flew in carrying Tom Estes (9th SRW operations officer), three mission planners and Beale's best intelligence and maintenance personnel. At 0600 hrs a secure tele-printer clattered out details of the first sortie. It was to be flown just 22 hours later.

The first major problem to arise when the aircrew met with the mission planners centred on the paucity of diversionary fields available to the SR-71. Later that morning, the Mildenhall tanker reached Griffiss, and the unit's technicians began preparing 64-17979 for the jet's longest operational sortie to date. By mid-afternoon someone suggested that the crew should get some sleep since they had been up for 36 hours, and they would soon be airborne for another 16 hours during the sortie itself. They were directed to an old Base Officers' Quarters, where they found their rooms to be hot and the beds uncomfortable. Gary Coleman recalled, 'No one could snore like Jim Shelton, and I got no sleep at all, but I consoled myself with the thought that my pilot was getting some solid rest!'

The belligerent attitude of usually helpful European allies required JP-7 fuel and tanker crews to be hastily re-positioned from Mildenhall and Incirlik, in Turkey, to Zaragoza, in Spain. The lack of emergency landing sites was also proving to be a problem that appeared impossible to solve. Nevertheless, Jim Shelton cranked 64-17979's engines on cue and took off from Griffiss at 0200 hrs on 13 October on the first of nine *Giant Reach/ Busy Pilot* missions. He successfully completed the first of six aerial refuellings (two tankers in each air refuelling track) off the Gulf of St Lawrence ('Old Barge East'). Having topped-off, 64-17979 then accelerated and climbed east, en route for the next cell of tankers awaiting the thirsty 'Habu' off the coast of Portugal ('Rota East').

'Habu' was the name given to the SR-71 by its crews, this moniker having originated when the jet first deployed operationally to Kadena air base, on the Japanese island of Okinawa. The Habu is a long, dark and poisonous pit viper indigenous to the island.

Returning again to speed and altitude, the crew made a high-Mach dash through the Straits of Gibraltar and let down for a third aerial refuelling south of Crete ('Crete East'). Due to the tanker track's proximity to the war zone and Libya, the US Navy provided a CAP (Combat Air Patrol) from carrier-based Phantom IIs on station in the Mediterranean. 64-17979 then resumed its climb and acceleration to coast in over Port Said. Gary Coleman recalled;

'There was no indication of anything launched against us, but everyone was painting us on their radars as we made our turn inbound. The DEF panel lit up like a pinball machine, and I said to Jim, "This should be interesting".'

The Sun moves across the face of the earth at about 1000 mph. So if, during a west bound flight at Mach 3.2, an SR-71 was turned to the north or south, causing the sun to set, it could be made to reappear again – thus rising in the west – once the crew resumed their westbound heading! (Lockheed)

The fourth operational sortie flown by the 9th SRW during the Yom Kippur War was completed by this aircraft, SR-71A 64-17964. The jet susbequently flew its second, and final, mission over the Middle East battlefields on 2 December 1973 (*Paul F Crickmore*)

In all 64-17979 spent 25 minutes over 'denied territory', entering Egyptian airspace at 1103 hrs GMT. During this time the crew covered the Israeli battlefronts with both Egypt and Syria, before coasting out and letting down for their fourth aerial refuelling ('Crete West'), the track for which was still being capped by the US Navy. The crew's next 'hot leg' was punctuated by a fifth refuelling again off Portugal ('Rota West'), but the tankers from Zaragoza had difficulty getting a clearance through the busy offshore airway that was filled with civilian airliners – they could not request a priority clearance because of the secrecy of their mission. When approval was at last received, the air traffic controllers hesitated clearing the tanker cell on their requested track because 'unidentified high speed traffic, height unknown', was approaching from their '12 o'clock' position. The tankers could not reveal that the 'traffic' was actually their trade.

Soon after completing his mid-ocean refuelling, Shelton climbed and accelerated in 64-17979 for his final high-speed run across the western Atlantic towards New York. Mindful of his own fatigue, Gary Coleman was in awe of his pilot, who completed a textbook sixth aerial refuelling ('Old Barge West'), before 'greasing' the SR-71 back down at Griffiss after a combat sortie that had lasted 10 hours and 18 minutes (more than five hours of which was spent at Mach 3 or above). 64-17979 had been supported in its endeavours by no fewer than 14 ever-dependable KC-135Qs – four from Goose Bay, in Canada, two from Griffiss and eight from Torrejon, in Spain.

The crew's reconnaissance 'take' was of 'high quality', and it provided intelligence and defence analysts with much needed information concerning the disposition of Arab forces (and Soviet equipment) in the region, which was in turn made available to the Israelis.

WAR CONTINUES

The Syrian military situation was swinging in favour of the Israelis by 14 October. The Soviets had stepped up an airlift of military equipment and were aware that the Syrian front was collapsing. Washington had also begun supporting Israel with a huge airlift of US war materials. President Richard Nixon had requested $2.2 billion in emergency aid for the Israelis, and this move had in turn incensed Abu Dhabi, Libya and Qatar, who, as members of the Organisation of the Petroleum Exporting Countries (OPEC), had been meeting with oil companies in Vienna since 12 October. They immediately imposed a complete oil embargo on the US, and this move was quickly followed by other OPEC members.

To further warn other nations against supporting Israel, OPEC unilaterally announced a 70 per cent rise in oil prices and a five per cent per month cut in production. The decision caused panic in Western Europe, which depended on the Arab states for 80 per cent of its oil supply.

Meanwhile, in the Sinai desert the Egyptians launched a 100,000 strong offensive toward the east on 14 October – the result of this attack was one of the biggest tank battles in history. As Israeli forces repelled the offensive and gained ground, they established a bridgehead west of the Suez Canal that threatened to cut off the Egyptian army. With the Egyptian military situation becoming more and more precarious, President Nixon announced that US forces across the globe had been placed on military alert following receipt of information indicating that the Soviet Union was planning 'to send a very substantial force to the Middle East to relieve the beleaguered Egyptian Third Army, now completely encircled in the Sinai'.

This tense period in superpower relations was somewhat defused when Soviet Secretary Leonid Brezhnev supported a United Nations motion on 24 October that would eventually end the Yom Kippur War. Meanwhile, SR-71 surveillance missions continued.

At 0200 hrs on 25 October, Capt Al Joersz and Maj John Fuller got airborne from Griffiss in 64-17979 and overflew the Yom Kippur war zone for a second time. However, due to protestations from the Spanish government, the second and fifth aerial refuelling tracks were re-positioned off the coast of the Azores (and thus out of range of Spanish radars) and renamed 'Lajes East' and 'Lajes West'.

Concerned that the USSR might deploy personnel and equipment in support of their Arab allies, the US intelligence community tasked this SR-71 mission with the priority

Lined-up ready for an early morning take-off, 64-17979 completed the first non-stop mission from Griffiss to the Middle East and back on 13 October 1973. This aircraft completed no fewer than six of the nine SR-71 endurance sorties undertaken during *Giant Reach/ Busy Pilot* (*Paul F Crickmore*)

objective of monitoring port facilities at Latakia and Tartus, in Syria, and Port Said and Alexandria, in Egypt.

A third mission was chalked up by the same aircraft eight days later when, on 2 November, Majs Bob Helt and Larry Elliott secured more photography of the ports for national intelligence users. The crew also targeted Cairo International airport and the nearby Tura cave facilities, which it was believed might contain Soviet 'Scud-B' mobile surface-to-surface ballistic missiles and their launchers.

Maj Jim Wilson and RSO Capt Bruce Douglass performed their first Mediterranean sortie in 64-17964 on 11 November, the 10 hour 49 minute flight departing from Griffiss but terminating as planned at Seymour Johnson AFB, in North Carolina. The 9th SRW detachment had migrated to the south so as to avoid the worsening New York winter weather. Col Don Walbrecht headed up the new detachment that had been pre-arranged with HQ Tactical Air Command by Col Harlan Hain from the SAC Strategic Reconnaissance Center (SRC).

With the shooting war in the Middle East now over, SR-71 reconnaissance flights were used to verify compliance with the ceasefire agreement, and provide irrefutable photographic evidence of this to Secretary of State Henry Kissinger and his team, who were leading the delicately balanced withdrawal negotiations between deeply distrusting Israelis and Arabs.

Fierce fighting broke out along the ceasefire line on 30 November, and this threatened to destroy the fragile agreement brokered by the US government. Two days later, Majs Jim Sullivan and Noel Widdifield flew 64-17964 across the Atlantic to look at the situation on the ground. It proved to be a well-timed move as fighting had also begun that same day in the Golan Heights. Further diplomatic pressures put an end to the new skirmishes before Majs Pat Bledsoe and Reg Blackwell went out in 64-17979 on 10 December for another look at the positions held by the belligerents. They flew their 'clockwork' ten-hour mission and arrived back at Seymour Johnson 'on the minute' of their flight plan. Thereafter, things were quiet for the next five weeks, so the 'Beale Troops' went home for Christmas. They returned to North Carolina in January to continue with their Sinai surveillance activities, however.

On 25 January, Majs Buck Adams and Bill Machorek flew another perfect ten-hour sortie, but when they returned to Seymour Johnson they were faced with very low ceiling and visibility condition that 'mandated' a diversion to Griffiss. This would have put the urgently needed photographic 'take' out of position for processing. Col Walbrecht remembered;

'We had Buck grab some fuel from the standby tanker and jacked the ceiling up a bit – despite the protestations of Harlon Hain at SAC headquarters. Buck snuck in and made a perfect landing at Seymour Johnson under the lowest ceiling an SR-71 has ever landed beneath.'

The success of international peace efforts soon began to show. On 18 January 1974 a military

On 2 December 1973, Maj Jim Sullivan, with his RSO Maj Noel Widdifield, flew 64-17964 across the Atlantic to look at the situation on the ground in the Middle East. It proved to be a well-timed flight, as fighting had also begun that same day in the Golan Heights between Syrian and Israeli troops (USAF)

separation agreement was signed between Egyptian and Israeli defence officials that led to troop withdrawals. By mid-February the peace process was beginning to go into overdrive, and on the 18th four Arab nations proposed a truce in the Golan Heights. To verify the pullback, 64-17971 was dispatched to the Suez Canal on 25 January.

There had been a great deal of suspicion on both sides that the opposing forces would not pull back their troops. Consequently, the SR-71's imagery became the instrument of verification, and this was shown at the peace negotiations as proof. With the evidence in hand, diplomatic ties were restored between Egypt and the US after a break lasting seven years.

As troop withdrawals continued Majs T Y Judkins and G T Morgan flew 64-17979 on the penultimate sortie to the region. Appropriately, this evergreen aircraft also flew the final mission on 6 April 1974. It had undertaken two-thirds of the nine 'ten-hour' *Giant Reach/ Busy Pilot* sorties, chalking up a remarkable rate of success despite the very demanding nature of the missions.

Indeed, the 9th SRW as a whole had managed to perform all the tasks demanded of it without its highly complex aircraft suffering ground or air aborts or diversions. These nine missions represented a pinnacle of operational professionalism for the wing. They were a tribute not only to the dedication of the aircrews involved, but also to that of the staff planners and the small group of ground technicians who maintained the SR-71s away from home. These sorties stood as a testament to the long reach of the aircraft, and its ability to operate with impunity in a sophisticated, high threat environment.

Col Don Walbrecht (front, third from left) headed-up the SR-71 detachment that flew sorties into the Middle East from Seymour Johnson AFB, North Carolina. The three crews in the second row consist of Capt Bruce Douglass (RSO), Maj Jim Wilson (pilot), Capt Al Joersz (pilot), Maj John Fuller (RSO), Maj Randy Hertzog (pilot) and Maj John Carnochan (RSO) (*USAF via Don Walbrecht*)

Col Pat Halloran had also initially led the 9th SRW det when it moved from Griffiss to Seymour Johnson in early November 1973. He is seen here posing with his troops for an official detachment photograph soon after arriving at the North Carolina base (*USAF*)

GIANT REACH

Operation *Giant Reach* was Strategic Air Command's codename for Europe-based contingency planning for SR-71 Photo Intelligence (PHOTINT) and Electronic Intelligence (ELINT) reconnaissance gathering missions. SAC's original plan had been to split this coverage and conduct both PHOTINT and ELINT of the Middle East and purely ELINT of Eastern Europe. It was thought that the PHOTINT mission would be virtually impossible to conduct on a regular basis in the latter region because of the traditionally poor weather conditions that often blighted northern latitudes.

In order to validate these contingency plans, which were initially published by HQ SAC on 6 April 1970, five KC-135Qs would firstly have to be deployed to Incirlik air base. Once they were in place, an SR-71, together with three more KC-135Qs carrying both fuel and support personnel, would be assigned to Torrejon on a 30-day TDY basis. However, the Spanish government prohibited overt reconnaissance flights originating from or recovering into bases in their country. Consequently, that element of the proposal was altered so that the SR-71 would be based at RAF Mildenhall instead.

During the early planning phase of *Giant Reach* it was thought that the SR-71 would conduct between six and eight sorties during each deployment, and the photo-product generated by the aircraft would be processed by the 497th Reconnaissance Technical Group (RTG) at Shierstein, in West Germany. ELINT and High Resolution Radar (HRR) 'take' would be ferried back to Beale and analysed by the 9th Reconnaissance Technical Squadron (RTS). The additional funds required to support such operations were not initially available, however. Despite this, HQ USAF directed SAC to spend a modest $50,000 from its Operation and Maintenance budget on alterations to the apron adjacent to Hanger 538 at Mildenhall as a precautionary measure should the Joint Chiefs of Staff (JCS) direct that such sorties should go ahead. This construction work was completed in 1971.

As noted in the previous chapter, the first operational requirement generated for a series of European-based SR-71 sorties occurred on 6 October 1973 with the outbreak of the Yom Kippur War. With the UK

On 1 September 1974, SR-71 64-17972 established a new transatlantic world speed record from London to New York of just 1 hour 54 minutes and 56 seconds – it stands to this day. Having completed the speed run, the crew recovered into Farnborough, where the jet was the star attraction at that year's airshow (*Bob Archer*)

government refusing to allow the 9th SRW to operate from RAF bases at the time, it was not until 1 September 1974 that the first 'Habu' visited Britain. On that historic date, Majs Jim Sullivan and Noel Widdifield, in SR-71A 64-17972, established a transatlantic world speed record from New York to London of less than two hours – a record that still stands to this day. Four days later, Capt 'Buck' Adams and Maj Bill Machorek also set a record during the aircraft's return trip to Los Angeles of less than four hours.

To underline the partnership status of any future SR-71 deployments to the UK, Secretary of State Henry Kissinger instructed Mrs Anne Armstrong, the US Ambassador to Britain, to inform Her Majesty's Government that the US 'would of course be prepared to share with the British information produced by such SR-71 missions'.

Detailed route planning for any future SR-71 deployments to the UK was conducted by the SRC. It would send details of three proposed tracks to the 98th Strategic Wing (SW) at Torrejon, as this unit was responsible for directing SAC operations from Mildenhall. Detachment 1 of the 98th SW, stationed at the UK base, then coordinated all necessary prior actions, notifications and clearances with the appropriate British officials.

On 20 April 1976, two KC-135Qs and the same SR-71 (64-17972) that had established the transatlantic speed records almost two years

Majs Jim Sullivan (left) and RSO Noel Widdifield (right) were the crew of 64-17972 on 1 September 1974 – the day the first SR-71 landed on British soil (*USAF*)

Capt Harold Adams and Maj William Machorek were scheduled to fly 64-17972 back to Beale AFB on 12 September 1974, but a technical malfunction with the aircraft delayed their departure from Mildenhall by one day (*Bob Archer*)

With all systems 'code one', Adams and Machorek depart Mildenhall on 13 September. They established the current world speed record between London and Los Angeles of 3 hours 47 minutes and 35 seconds during the return flight to Beale (*USAF via Art-Tech/Aerospace*)

earlier returned to the UK, but this time the trip was made without the attendant media coverage that had accompanied its previous brief visit. Using the call sign 'Burns 31', Majs 'Pat' Bledsoe and John Fuller completed the flight from Beale to Mildenhall in 4 hours and 42 minutes.

The key objective of this deployment was for the aircraft to complete two training sorties, the first of which was to be flown over both the North Sea and the Norwegian Sea, and the second over the English Channel and the Bay of Biscay. These flights would both exercise the aircraft's base support facilities and help to shape the SR-71's flight profile and operating procedures that would need to be adopted when flying in the cramped and congested airspace of Northern Europe. Such missions would then pave the way for future SR-71 participation in NATO training exercises, the first of which was scheduled for later that same year.

Three days after the aircraft's arrival, the first evaluation sortie got underway when Capts Maury Rosenberg and Don Bulloch engaged both 'burners and departed the base. However, as they cruised along the west coast of Norway at an altitude of 72,000 ft, Bulloch noticed that the outside air temperature was 30°C warmer than had been anticipated. After quickly re-calculating the aircraft's performance values in this sub-Arctic environment by cross-correlating exhaust gas temperature (EGT) against engine air inlet door position, and interpolating the aircraft's true airspeed from the astro-inertial navigation system, the crew were alarmed to learn that their computed fuel specifics were way off the mark.

In fact their actual fuel burn was so much higher than that calculated by the nav-planners back at Mildenhall that 64-17972 was going to be 8000 lbs lighter on JP-7 than had been scheduled by the time it arrived at its air refuelling control point (ARCP). This in turn meant that the jet would barely be able to reach the two KC-135Qs. The crew prudently decided to abort the mission and return to Mildenhall instead.

The second, and final, southerly-orientated training sortie was completed by Bledsoe and Fuller on 28 April, and two days later, using the call sign 'Kabab 31', Rosenberg and Bulloch returned 64-17972 to Beale.

EXERCISES

Five months later, two large NATO exercises commenced in Western Europe. *Cold Fire 76* was a land and air operation than ran from 7 to 10 September in West Germany, whilst *Teamwork 76* involved land, sea and air assets exercising in the North and Norwegian Seas from 10 to 23 September. HQ European Command was keen that the SR-71 should participate in both exercises, pointing out that not only would this provide invaluable training and logistical experience for the 9th SRW, but that it would also demonstrate 'positive US resolve in support of NATO'.

Such participation would of course require authorisation from several command authorities, as well as the UK MoD, the Joint Chiefs of Staff (JCS), United States Air Forces Europe (USAFE) and NATO member nations. Luckily, negotiations to obtain prior approval for the SR-71 to overfly NATO countries and enter their airspace had already begun. As it turned out, the process was far from straightforward, and it took several months to complete – Denmark took it right to the wire, being the final country to grant its approval in early September.

The deployment of aircraft 64-17962 began on 2 September 1976, but Majs Al Cirino and Bruce Liebman (RSO) had to divert into Goose Bay air base, in Labrador, en route when the jet suffered engine trouble over the central United States. An emergency maintenance team was hastily despatched from Beale and the flight to Mildenhall was completed by Cirino and Liebman four days later. Majs Rich Graham and Don Emmons flew the aircraft the following day in support of *Teamwork 76*, the crew incorporating lessons learned from the previous deployment in April. They successfully completed their mission over the North and Norwegian Seas, before recovering safely back to 'The Hall'. Cirino and Liebman then flew a sortie into West Germany in support of *Cold Fire 76*, which 64-17962 completed satisfactorily.

Six missions were undertaken in total, and HRR imagery, standard photos and ELINT were collected from the exercise areas before Graham and Emmons flew the aircraft home after a European tour lasting 19 days.

Prior to the next 'Habu' deployment to the UK taking place, a change in SAC's European reporting structure took place following Senate ratification of a new treaty with the Spanish government in January 1976. The agreement stipulated a reduced American military presence in the country, which in turn meant deactivation of the 98th SW on 31 December 1976. Command of SAC assets based in Europe was duly transferred to the 306th SW, which had been activated four months earlier and co-located with HQ USAFE at Ramstein air base, in West Germany.

Gen Richard Ellis, Commander in Chief USAFE, and CINCSAC, Gen Russell Dougherty (whom Gen Ellis would succeed as the SAC commander on 1 August 1977), had had extensive discussions in the months leading up to this command re-structure, and had formulated a plan that would have a profound impact on the build up of SAC assets in Europe. It had been decided that the 306th SW commander would report directly to CINCSAC and his staff, and that he had 'delegated authority' to exercise the CINCSAC's command responsibilities for allpresent and future SAC European operations. The latter included the European Tanker Force, the RC-135s that were TDY with the 306th SW's detachments at Mildenhall and Hellenikon air base, in Greece, and any future B-52 or U-2R/ SR-71 deployments.

A number of the crews that flew the early SR-71 missions from Mildenhall in the latter half of the 1970s are visible in this photo, taken after Lt Col Jack Rogers had made his last flight in the 'Habu'. From the top row down, from left to right, are John Murphy, Joe Vida, Don Emmons, Al Cirino, Tom Allison, John Fuller, Rich Graham (on his own), 'Buzz' Carpenter, Bill Groninger and Bruce Leibman. Standing at left are Bill Keller, Chuck Sober, Joe Kinego (in pressure suit to left) and Roger Jacks. In the bottom row are Jim Sullivan, Jay Reid and Tom Keck. Standing to the right are B C Thomas, Pat Bledsloe and John Storrie (*USAF*)

64-17972 again visited the UK for a ten-day TDY on 20 April 1976 (*Paul F Crickmore*)

64-17962 first deployed to Mildenhall between 6-18 September 1976. It is seen here during its second, and final, deployment, which saw the aircraft assigned to Det 4 from 19 October 1984 through to mid-October 1985. The SR-71 is flanked by two RAF Jaguars from RAF Coltishall-based No 41 Sqn (*Crown Copyright*)

The desire to increase SAC's presence in Europe had its roots in the changing nature of the Soviet/Warsaw Pact threat facing NATO. Gen Ellis wanted B-52s to deploy periodically to England, together with their support tankers, in order to train such a force to a level that was capable of performing a wartime tactical mission. This, he envisaged, would consist of interdiction both in the vicinity of the battle area and beyond its forward edge, airfield attack, defence suppression, sea surveillance and anti-shipping. It followed, therefore, that if B-52s were tasked to perform a mission similar in nature to that which they had flown for eight years in Southeast Asia, the U-2R and SR-71 would again be required to provide complementary pre-strike and bomb damage assessment (BDA) imagery, in addition to Signals Intelligence (SIGINT) warning information.

An additional issue of particular concern to Gen Ellis was the unprecedented level of sophistication that accompanied the twice-yearly Soviet/Warsaw Pact exercises that had began on 31 December 1976. Specifically he noted, 'Of particular interest to us at SAC is their coordinated and extensive use of airborne command posts as alternate command centres, and their ability to control forces when required, particularly during/after a global nuclear exchange'. On balance, therefore, it is perhaps not surprising that as far as Gen Ellis was concerned, it was 'most desirous' that the SR-71 and U-2R deploy to RAF Mildenhall to monitor these exercises.

The third SR-71 training deployment to the UK was completed by 64-17958, which arrived as 'Ring 21' on 7 January 1977 again with Maj Rich Graham at the helm and Maj Don Emmons 'in the back'. In support, two KC-135Qs flew in 65 maintenance, operations and logistics specialists, together with 80,000 lbs of equipment. 9th SRW CO Col John Storrie also accompanied the deployment in order to inspect Mildenhall's support facilities for himself.

This ten-day deployment was timed to coincide with the approximate date of President Jimmy Carter's inauguration, and it would thereby underline the United States' continued support of its NATO allies.

Two training sorties were again flown by the SR-71, covering the same areas as the April 1976 deployment. Majs Tom Allison and J T Vida (RSO) made up the second crew on this det, and they repositioned the aircraft back to Beale as 'Paver 86' on 17 January.

In late February 1977, HQ SAC proposed to the JCS that it seek approval for the SR-71's first ever operational deployment to Europe. It was proposed that the 17-day tour should consist of one training sortie, similar to the two completed in January 1977, and two Peacetime Aerial Reconnaissance Programme (PARPRO) missions. The first of these would be a coordinated sortie with a Mildenhall-based RC-135V along the Barents Sea periphery, while the second mission would be flown over West Germany. SAC requested that both of the PARPRO missions be approved to collect ELINT and HRR imagery, since they were particularly anxious to demonstrate the unique characteristics of the latter to other potential national intelligence users – specifically the US Army and US Navy.

Whilst the proposal navigated its way through the JCS evaluation process, the SRC worked on preparing the aircraft's tracks in anticipation of receiving an affirmative for the deployment. The JCS duly issued SAC with the necessary authorisation to proceed on 6 May 1977. It also instructed that the SR-71 was to adhere to tracks prepared earlier in the year by the SRC, as these had been used by the State Department to coordinate and obtain the necessary clearances from the five NATO nations through whose airspace the SR-71 would fly. The JCS also went on to direct HQ SAC to deploy a Mobile Processing Center (MPC), held in storage at Beale, to Mildenhall. This last instruction was issued in response to a request from Gen Ellis, and as such had been anticipated by SAC.

MPC

In 1977, two MPCs existed. In addition to the one alluded to by the JCS, the other (MPC I) was in caretaker status at Kadena air base. Each MPC consisted of 24 trailer-like vans that measured 8 ft x 8 ft x 40 ft, and collectively they contained all the equipment necessary to process raw intelligence data collected by the SR-71's HRR and cameras. MPC I was also equipped with an Electro-Magnetic Reconnaissance (EMR) formatter that processed the ELINT tapes. However, at a cost of over a million dollars each (mid-1960s values), it had been decided that only one MPC would have this additional EMR capability.

The MPC could be deployed overseas in various tailored packages or van combinations to support different levels and types of reconnaissance operation. The complete package was designed to support one SR-71 mission per day, and required an operating staff of 60 officers, airmen and civilian contractors. Depending on the amount of data collected, typically photography and HRR imagery was available to the interpreters four hours after the 'Habu' had landed. MPC I also afforded top-line ELINT signals ready for first stage analysis in about three hours.

The entire 24-van package of MPC II, destined for Mildenhall, weighed in at 290,000 lbs, and was transported to the UK in two C-5s and four C-141s. Transportation costs were picked-up by USAFE, but manpower and payment for expendable supplies came from SAC monies already allocated. On arrival in the UK, MPC II was located inside a secure compound within Hangar 538 at the base, and at great credit to all involved, the facility was operational when 'Indy 69' (64-17958) touched-down at Mildenhall on 16 May 1977. Majs 'Buzz' Carpenter

64-17972 visited the UK on no fewer than six occasions between September 1974 and July 1983. It is seen here in low-vis markings during its final deployment to Det 4, which ran from 18 December 1982 through to 6 July 1983 (*Paul F Crickmore*)

and John Murphy had taken off from Beale at 0200 hrs, refuelled twice and flown two hot legs during their four-hour flight, prior to arriving safely at the UK base in the middle of the afternoon.

These missions were supposedly secret, and therefore had to be coordinated ahead of time through various Federal Aviation Agency (FAA) offices and regional Air Traffic Control Centres (ATCCs) – a process also replicated through Canadian ATCCs. By following such procedures, SAC hoped to safeguard the SR-71's intended route and keep the jet's ultimate destination a secret from those not dialled into the mission. Maj Carpenter recalled;

'About 150 miles from Beale, out over the Nevada desert, we hooked up with our awaiting tankers at 25,000 ft. During the refuelling we took on about 60,000 lbs of fuel and dropped off the tanker over northern Utah, at which point we started our climb and acceleration. Passing through 60,000 ft, we would routinely call the ATCC, as we usually turned off our electronic altitude reporting equipment at this point. Salt Lake Center replied to our call with "Roger 'Indy 69'. Have a great time in Jolly Old England". So much for mission security!

'The cruise leg was uneventful as we passed over the northern United States and into Canadian airspace at Mach 3.0 and above 75,000 ft. It was a moonless night, which when flying over areas thinly populated gave you an opportunity to see a vast array of twinkling stars that you don't usually see on the ground because of their lack of intensity and filtering by the atmosphere.

'As we approached the east coast of Canada near Goose Bay, Labrador, the sun was starting to rise as we were descending and decelerating. This was wonderful to view from 75,000 ft, yet it made for a difficult refuellings, because as you were under the tanker at 25,000 ft, trying to maintain your position and monitor the refuelling director lights on the belly of the KC-135, the sun was just above the horizon and right in your eye-line. It blinded you, even with your helmet sun visor down.

'With the refuelling done, we then separated from the tanker again and started our climb and acceleration eastward over the Atlantic and on into Scotland. As we crossed, Greenland was partly visible and a couple of huge icebergs were seen slowly floating south. Iceland was completely shrouded in cloud as usual, and the weather in England was going to be overcast and wet. Our descent and deceleration was normal, and it brought us over

England at subsonic speed. Proceeding south and east to Mildenhall, we made contact with our mobile crew for recovery – Majs Tom Allison and J T Vida – about 50 miles out. They advised us of the weather, and to look for the "birdwatchers". Initially John and I were puzzled by the "birdwatchers" remark. As it turned out, about half-an-hour before our arrival, a couple of hundred aircraft "birdwatchers" showed up with their cameras and zoom lenses to photograph our arrival – again, so much for the secretive nature of our flight over. The "birdwatcher" net sure trumped our security plan.

'Arrival was uneventful, and after a precision approach I chose to take the aircraft around for one visual approach. I could see the "birdwatchers" with their cameras at all the choice spots around the airfield fence – some even waved to us as we taxied to our parking hangar!'

On 18 May 64-17958 satisfactorily completed the JCS-directed training sortie over the North Sea. The aircraft was configured with the same sensor package that it would carry aloft during the two operational missions, namely the nose-mounted HRR, ELINT sensors in the two aft mission bays (bays S and T) and a full DEF system.

FIRST OPERATIONAL MISSION

On 20 May 1977, SR-71 64-17958 made history when it undertook the first operational mission by a Mildenhall-based 'Habu'. Its pilot for the flight was Maj Tom Allison, who recalled;

'J T Vida – my RSO – and I arrived at Mildenhall via a KC-135Q, along with the TDY Detachment Commander, Col Willie Lawson, and the Nav/Planner, Lt Col Red Winters. This particular mission was tasked at the Top Secret level using HRR imagery and ELINT sensors against the Soviet submarine base at Murmansk, on the Barents Sea. It was also scheduled as a coordinated mission with an RC-135V "Rivet Joint".

'It was a little unusual for a PARPRO mission to be classified Top Secret, but J T and I thought that this was because it was a coordinated sortie, and one of the first to go into the area around Murmansk. It may also have been due to the fact that the Soviets had deployed SA-5 SAMs around Murmansk, thus making this mission one of the first occasions that the SR-71 had been used in an area where there were known SA-5s. The latter was a much more capable SAM than the earlier SA-2, which was also widely deployed in the USSR, and was not considered to pose any great threat to the "Habu".

'During the mission planning session on 19 May, it was discovered that the Soviets had issued a Notice To Airman (NOTAM) warning of SAM test firing to altitudes in excess of 100,000 ft. The coordinates for the NOTAM area were off the coast of Murmansk, and they nicely bracketed the only patch of sky that we would fly through twice during

Majs Tom Allison and J T Vida made history on 20 May 1977 when they performed the first operational mission undertaken by a Mildenhall-based SR-71. They flew 64-17958 on this occasion (*USAF*)

the mission – going in and coming out. We were always concerned about the Soviet military having intelligence pertaining to our missions prior to them actually being flown, and the issuing of this SAM NOTAM on the eve of our first operational sortie seemed like a highly improbable coincidence. Maybe, somehow, word about our mission had leaked out.

'Although at the time J T and I were not really aware of it, it seems that in some quarters this possible security leak caused quite a bit of concern. Apparently, there were several secure telephone conference calls made between RAF Mildenhall and the SAC SRC, and the discussion centred on whether or not to cancel the mission based on the NOTAM.

'It should be noted that the mission track was planned so that the SR-71 remained in international airspace at all times. If we stayed on the "black line" we would never enter Soviet airspace. However, that said, the mission objective was to obtain maximum information concerning the submarine activities and area defences in this region. At one point during the second pass through the area the "Habu" was planned to be heading directly at the submarine base, perpendicular to the coastline, at Mach 3.15. We would then commence a high banking turn that would put us parallel to the coastline but headed out of the area. That point was right in the centre of the "missile-firing box" outlined by the NOTAM!

'The concern at SAC HQ centred on whether the Soviets would actually fire an SA-5 against an aircraft in international airspace. "Intent" was always a key word in a situation like this. Another concern was that the SA-5 was new and relatively unknown in terms of radio frequency (RF) indications and performance. We were later told that Kelly Johnson (the design genius behind the Lockheed SR-71) actually participated in the telephone conference, and his position was that we should not fly the mission. In the end, however, it was determined that the sortie would be flown as scheduled.

'The following day we all got airborne on time – the RC-135V, the KC-135Qs and the "Habu". Our mission profile was normal through the refuellings, but as we began our climb and acceleration to Mach 3+ cruise prior to entering the target area, it became obvious that the outside air temperature was much higher than we expected, and were used to. This caused the climb/acceleration to be slower than normal. It was so hot, and

The S-200 (NATO designation SA-5 'Gammon') was a medium-to high-altitude mobile SAM designed, manufactured and deployed by the USSR from 1967 as a replacement for the highly successful SA-2. The S-200 system was designed to operate in coordination with Soviet interceptors, the latter guarding the approaches to SAM sites. The system was deployed in large numbers during the late 1970s and early 1980s. Indeed, by the mid-1980s, some 130 sites and 1950 mobile launchers were operational throughout the USSR and the Eastern Bloc. The S-200 had been replaced in Russian service by more modern SAM systems by 2001 (*FAS*)

Majs 'Buzz' Carpenter (left) and his RSO John Murphy conducted the SR-71's second operational mission from Mildenhall on 24 May 1977 (*USAF via 'Buzz' Carpenter*)

our performance so degraded, that at the point where we should have been level at Mach 3.15 and 75,000 ft, we were just passing 60,000 ft and still climbing at Mach 2.8. As J T and I were discussing our situation, he mentioned that the radar sensor had just come on. We had never had it come on while we were still climbing before. Additionally, the slower performance caused us to be well below the planned fuel curve. We had to decide whether to continue with the mission.

'In the event, we pressed on and finally levelled off at our desired cruise speed. We actually pushed the Mach up a little to try and help ourselves get back on the fuel curve – although I knew we would never be able to make up all of it, I was comfortable that we would be able to get back to the tankers for the next air refuelling if nothing else went wrong. And, in fact, that is just what happened. We completed both passes through the target area, and the missile firing warning area, with very little reaction noted on our defensive systems. The last air refuelling and the trip back to Mildenhall were uneventful, which was just the way we liked it.

'During the debriefing following the flight we received word that we had already had a very successful mission, and our "radar take" had not even been processed yet. It seemed that the RC-135V "Rivet Joint" that was in the target area for some time before we arrived had had quite a bit of Soviet company in the form of interceptors. Just as we were beginning to enter the area, the RC-135V crew became aware that the fighters had abruptly departed, and the linguists monitoring the radios overheard the Soviet ground control intercept controller trying to vector the interceptors onto the SR-71. At least one fighter pilot was heard to say, "I can see the contrail above and ahead. It is climbing at a very high speed and I will not be able to catch it". Heck, we already knew that!

'Further adding to the initial success of the mission was the first ever capture of RF signals associated with the SA-5, which were picked up by both our systems and the SIGINT equipment in the RC-135V. J T and I had spent 45 minutes in the "denied area", most of it at a little in excess of Mach 3 – just another day at the office.'

Four days later, Majs 'Buzz' Carpenter and John Murphy (RSO) performed the second operational mission to originate from Mildenhall in 64-17958. Carpenter recalled;

'John and I were tasked with flying the tricky German mission. Like the Baltic sortie, one could not fly the aircraft at Mach 3 and still hope to make the turns that allowed the jet to stay within the country border limits imposed upon us. In both cases, while flying at Mach 2.8 a maximum 45-degree bank high-angle turn was required to stay within the confines of the mission ground track. Because of aircraft energy management, a slight descent was sometimes required to maintain the 45° of bank and Mach 2.8. These turns were planned for 42°, which gave you an additional three degrees should this not be enough to maintain your critical ground track. However, the steeper the bank, the more likely the loss of altitude in the turn. If you were flying in warmer than standard air temperatures, this energy management balance was aggravated still further. Often, we would descend a couple of thousand feet just prior to commencing the turning in order to give ourselves an energy advantage.

'In an effort to keep the mission as secret as possible, the mobile crew would reaffirm our take-off time and physically tell us when our flight clearance was ready, rather than the Mildenhall Control Tower radioing us. With these checks complete, 30 minutes prior to take-off we would initiate our engine start and aircraft systems checks, without any radio calls. The tower would flash a light to signal our clearance to taxi and to enter the runway for take-off. With UK airspace deconfliction completed, a green light would be flashed to us from the tower and a radio-silent take-off would then occur.

'Traffic had been cleared from our path and we climbed unrestricted to 25,000 ft and headed out over the North Sea to meet our tankers. When the refuelling was completed, we executed a right turn to the southeast and initiated our climb and acceleration.

'Our entry target was to cross the German coast near Wilhelmshaven at Mach 2.8 above 70,000 ft. We were heading almost due south, towards Kaiserslautern, avoiding overflying major population areas. Below us most of the ground was covered with low clouds. This track was followed by a 30° bank turn to the southeast, passing southwest of Stuttgart and heading into Bavaria. Here, the cloud cover broke and the landscape was a wonderful patchwork of little villages, agricultural fields and mountainous terrain. Now came the difficult manoeuvre to ensure that we maintained our track inside West Germany while flying south around Munich as we executed a 45° high-bank turn. Luckily, there were some clouds below us, and the cooler than standard upper air temperatures enabled us to maintain our altitude.

Seen here during a training flight from Beale towards the end of its career, 64-17958 undertook two deployments to Mildenhall in 1977. It was in-country from 7 to 17 January and 16 to 31 May. The aircraft subsequently returned to Det 4 in 1981 and 1984 (*USAF*)

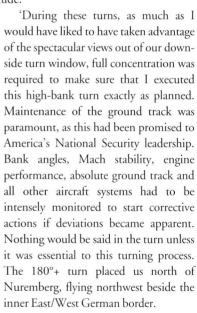

'During these turns, as much as I would have liked to have taken advantage of the spectacular views out of our downside turn window, full concentration was required to make sure that I executed this high-bank turn exactly as planned. Maintenance of the ground track was paramount, as this had been promised to America's National Security leadership. Bank angles, Mach stability, engine performance, absolute ground track and all other aircraft systems had to be intensely monitored to start corrective actions if deviations became apparent. Nothing would be said in the turn unless it was essential to this turning process. The 180°+ turn placed us north of Nuremberg, flying northwest beside the inner East/West German border.

'Basically, our sensors ran the whole time along the inner German border objective area. Once abeam Frankfurt, passing to the north, a turn north was then completed to align us with our departure track out of Germany that would see us flying across the same stretch of coast that we had entered over less than an hour earlier.

'Once clear of the coast, we started a 30° descending turn to the southwest. It took over 200 nautical miles to start a descent, decelerate and level off at 25,000 ft, inbound to England. There was not much margin for error, or any type of delay, in the close confines that we were operating in. This all happened very quickly, and descents were another high activity time period for the crew as we made sure that the aircraft maintained those narrow flight parameters to allow for a safe descent. Engine compressor stalls could occur with engine flameouts if your tight descent profile was not maintained.

'Once below Mach 2.4 the profile became more flexible, and at Mach 1.8, with the inlet spikes full forward, there was even more latitude. The profile of the descent was precisely planned so that the jet crossed over the coastline of the UK at subsonic speed.

'As we approached England, we would break radio silence for the first time during the entire mission and contact Northern Radar. We duly followed their guidance for an instrument recovery back at Mildenhall. UK ATC sector radar controllers and, when required, their precision radar approach controllers, were superb. This is probably because of all the practice they receive handling aircraft in England's notorious weather!

'At the end of an operational mission, a single approach full stop landing was always planned. After landing and deploying our huge orange drag 'chute, slowing was closely monitored. Once our speed was below 80 knots, the drag 'chute would be jettisoned if there was not a severe crosswind. As we taxied in in front of our parking hangar, the sensor crews were already in place to immediately download the recce equipment and process what we had collected as soon as we had stopped. As the engines were shut down, sensor crews began opening up the jet's hatches, and by the time John and I stepped from the cockpit most of the recording equipment had already been downloaded.

'We were usually debriefed planeside about the aircraft's systems and anything unusual that had arisen during the course of the mission, before we were driven back to the Physiological Support Division (PSD) building and de-suited. This was followed by extensive debriefs, and then it was our turn to assume the mobile back-up position for Tom and J T for their next scheduled mission.'

On 31 May 1977, Majs Allison and Vida redeployed 64-17958 back to Beale using the call sign 'Resay 35'.

64-17958 stayed at Mildenhall for 15 days in May 1977, before being returned to Beale as call sign 'Resay 35' at month end. The jet's high visibility titling and national insignia contrast markedly with those worn by 64-17958 in the photograph opposite, which was taken a decade later (*Bob Archer*)

MORE DEPLOYMENTS

I n an effort to improve command and control of its forces in Europe, and to further strengthen liaison between CINCSAC and US and Allied commanders in Europe, HQ SAC activated the 7th Air Division at Ramstein air base on 1 July 1978 as a direct reporting unit. It also moved 'on paper' the 306th SW from Ramstein to Mildenhall. Up until this date, the latter had been referred to as Detachment 1 of the 306th SW when operating from the UK base.

Even before the SR-71 had commenced its first operational deployment to Europe, planning was already underway for a second, which was scheduled for the autumn of 1977. Both NATO and USAFE commanders were anxious that the aircraft should again participate in exercise *Cold Fire*. However, reconnaissance specialists at HQ SAC were sceptical as to the value of such an exercise, mindful of the limitations imposed upon the jet's sensors when forced to adopt a restrictive flight profile in order to conform with political considerations based upon Switzerland, Austria and France's decision to deny it clearance to overfly their airspace.

However, the success of the first deployment ensured that the request made by Maj Gen Earl Peak (SAC Deputy Chief of Staff for Operations) to the JCS for an October/November deployment was approved. The year's second PARPRO det would record another first for the 9th SRW, as the 'Habu' was scheduled to conduct an operational sortie during the course of its positioning flight to Mildenhall. Taking off from Beale on 20 October 1977, the SR-71 would fly eastward over the Arctic Circle and perform a coordinated intelligence gathering sortie with RC-135U 'Combat Sent II' 64-14849 in the Barents Sea, before landing at Mildenhall. This particular RC-135U would fly 30 operational missions over the Baltic and Barents Seas during this, its second, or 'Papa', deployment, to Mildenhall in 1977.

An RC-135V 'Rivet Joint' aircraft is seen at Mildenhall supporting an SR-71 detachment in the late 1970s. All eight RC-135Vs were assigned to the 55th SRW, which called Offutt AFB, Nebraska, home. This aircraft was one of seven RC-135Cs upgraded to 'Rivet Joint 5' configuration in 1974-75 as part of the 'Big Safari' modification programme. 64-14845 is still in service with the 55th Wing today. Visible directly behind the RC-135V is EC-135H 61-0282 of the 10th Airborne Command and Control Squadron, which provided USCINCEUR with a survivable Airborne Command Post. Unlike the RC-135V and SR-71, this aircraft was permanently based at Mildenhall. It was retired from active service and redesignated a ground maintenance trainer in November 1991 (*Bob Archer*)

At this juncture, it might be useful to provide an overview concerning the vital role played by the RC-135V 'Rivet Joint' and RC-135U 'Combat Sent' platforms when operating in conjunction with the SR-71. The gathering of intelligence gleaned from the electromagnetic spectrum is known as Signals Intelligence, or SIGINT for short. This can be divided into two sub-categories, namely Communications Intelligence (COMINT), which is defined as the 'interception and processing of foreign communications passed by radio, wire or other electromagnetic means', and Electronic Intelligence (ELINT), which is the collection of 'information derived from foreign non-communications electromagnetic radiations emanating from other than atomic detonations or radioactive sources. This includes frequencies, signal strength, pulse lengths, pulse rates and other details of radars and electronic warfare equipment'.

Once such details have been collected, collated, identified and disseminated, it becomes possible to establish a potential adversary's Electronic Order of Battle (EOB). Then, once specific signal characteristics have been identified as belonging to particular radar types or electronic warfare equipment, it becomes possible to develop forms of Electronic Countermeasures (ECM), or indeed Electronic Counter-Countermeasures (ECCM), equipment that can jam the signal characteristics upon which such equipment is dependent, thereby degrading its effectiveness.

EOB data was gathered by a small fleet of highly sophisticated, air refuellable platforms specially developed by the USAF and designated RC-135s. By the late 1970s, the two principle variants performing this work were the 'hog-nosed' RC-135V 'Rivet Joint', which 'hoovered up' a vast array of data that enabled the types and locations of various sensors to be established, and the RC-135U 'Combat Sent'. The latter utilised its principal sensor – the power pattern measurement system – to perform fine grain analysis of radar signals from pre-determined locations.

This detailed intelligence was in turn supplied to agencies such as the Joint Strategic Target Planning Staff (JSTPS), which was co-located with HQ SAC. Both organisations would use the SIGINT to update the Single Integrated Operational Plan (SIOP) and to develop ECM equipment to counter Soviet radar threats.

Having an RC-135 fly a coordinated sortie with an SR-71 offered several benefits when it came to SIGINT collection. Firstly, thanks to the 'Habu's' high altitude performance, its sensors had the ability to gather SIGINT from sources operating up to 350 miles away from its position – well inside denied territory. Additionally, SAC reconnaissance specialists believed that the appearance of an SR-71 would stimulate the electromagnetic environment by eliciting an unusual response from Soviet defensive systems, provoking many more radars to be switched on to monitor the situation and more communication channels to be used.

The scheduled 20 October mission was, in the event, delayed for four days due to bad weather at Thule air base, in Greenland – the SR-71's nominated emergency recovery base for this deployment. Finally, on 24 October Capt Joe Kinego and his RSO Maj Larry Elliott completed the 5 hour 49 minute mission to Mildenhall in 64-17976. During the sortie, Kinego initially conducted a post take-off fuel top-up near Edmonton, in Saskatchewan, followed by a second aerial refuelling near Greenland and a third after the Barents Sea 'take' off the coast of Norway.

On its 24 October 1977 flight to the UK from Beale, 64-17976 conducted a coordinated reconnaissance gathering mission with an RC-135U 'Combat Sent II' aircraft over the Barents Sea. Note the Playboy bunnie emblem chalked onto the SR-71's tail – a logo usually associated with SR-71 64-17978, which was christened 'The Rapid Rabbit' (*Bob Archer*)

After departing Mildenhall on a monitoring sortie into West Germany, the SR-71 crew would first head for the initial Air Refuelling Control Point (ARCP) over The Wash and take on additional JP-7 from an ever reliable KC-135Q tanker. (*via Paul F Crickmore*)

The 9th SRW planned to fly several more sorties than had previously been undertaken on UK deployments up to that point, and two additional 'Habu' crews arrived accordingly via KC-135Q tanker. The men selected to gain valuable operational experience in this unique environment were Majs Bob Crowder and Jack Veth, together with their respective RSOs John Morgan and Bill Keller. Between the three crews, eight round-robin sorties were flown into Germany, these occurring on 27 and 29 October and 1, 3, 6, 7, 10 and 11 November.

The average mission time for these sorties was 2 hours and 38 minutes, and involved one air refuelling shortly after take-off over The Wash – a large bay like area, located off the northern coast of East Anglia. The route consisted of just a single pass along track X-027, which was aligned parallel to the East German/Czechoslovakian borders specifically to monitor the Soviet/Warsaw Pac autumn troop rotation. HQ Europe Command (EUCOM) requested that SAC direct the SR-71 to collect as varied an ELINT/HRR sampling as possible. Consequently, the 3 November mission saw the SR-71 launch after sunset and complete a night sortie – a practice seldom undertaken due to noise considerations.

Yet another milestone was achieved during the 'Habu's' redeployment back to Beale when, on 16 November, as 'Dew 49', Majs Bob Crowder and John Morgan took 64-17976 on an outbound intelligence-gathering mission. Having left Mildenhall, Crowder topped-off over the North Sea and then conducted another coordinated sortie with RC-135U 'Combat

Sent II' 64-14849. The 'Habu' spent 45 minutes collecting intelligence in the constrained geography of the Baltic Sea, before a second aerial refuelling was completed off the north coast of Scotland and a third off the east coast of North America. The jet eventually touched down at Beale after a flight lasting 6 hours and 11 minutes.

To optimise the full potential of this mission, the SRC had provided the 'Combat Sent II' crew with specific instructions as to the SR-71's altitude, track, speed and target timings so that the RC-135U could complement the SR-71's track profile. Although the crew manoeuvred their aircraft precisely in accordance with the SRC's collection plan, one particularly sought after signal – the identity of which is still classified today – unfortunately remained elusive.

On 24 April 1978, Majs Jay Murphy and RSO John Billingsley deployed 64-17964 to Mildenhall to cover the Soviet spring troop rotations. During its 16-day stay, two crews flew the aircraft prior to Majs Bob Crowder and John Morgan ferrying it back to Beale on 12 May.

US NAVY INTEREST

Bordered by Finland and Norway to the west, the Kola Peninsula extends in a southeasterly direction into the Barents Sea. This area was of intense interest to Adm James L Holloway III, Chief of Naval Operations (CNO), because the five naval bases at Zapadnya Litsa, Vidyayevo, Gadzhievo, Severomorsk and Gremikha were home to the largest and

Majs Jay Murphy and John Billingsley deployed 64-17964 to Mildenhall on 24 April 1978. This 'open air' scene is typical of early deployments before dedicated hangerage for the SR-71 had been constructed at the base. Note the dark green Buick start cart used to crank the engine parked under the aircraft's left wing (Bob Archer)

Photographed on 24 October 1977, RC-135U 64-14849 climbs out from Mildenhall en route to the Barents Sea for a coordinated sortie with Capt Joe Kinego and Maj Larry Elliott in 64-17976. This same aircraft also participated in '976's' coordinated sortie over the Baltic on 16 November. Again assigned to the 55th SRW, 64-14849 was the last of just three RC-135Us created for the USAF through the modification of a trio of RC-135Cs under the 'Big Safari' programme in 1971. A veteran of the Vietnam War, it too is still serving with the 55th Wing today (Bob Archer)

most powerful of the Soviet Union's three fleets – the Northern Fleet. It controlled two-thirds of the entire Soviet nuclear submarine force – over 100 vessels in all – the majority of which were based in the Kola Gulf area because the warming influence of the North Atlantic Drift meant that these important ports remained ice-free all year round.

By the spring of 1978, a group of US Navy Intelligence analysts had become increasingly concerned at what appeared to be a fundamental shift in Soviet naval strategy. Virtually since the start of the Cold War, when the 'Soviet Bear began to swim', American planners believed that the Soviet Navy was bent on challenging the United States on the high seas, and that should war break out Soviet attack submarines would attempt to sink US shipping re-supplying Europe, just as the German U-boat fleet had done in World War 2.

However, it now seemed increasingly likely to these analysts that the Soviets were on the cusp of knocking over a cornerstone of US nuclear strategy, as they believed that Soviet 'boomers' were now being protected by attack submarines and surface vessels. They also believed that the powerful Northern Fleet was intent on establishing the entire Barents Sea as a 'no go' area for US and NATO navies. From their ice-free enclave, the submarines could slip from their berths at any time of the year and move into the Barents Sea. Once here, they could take up firing positions and launch their lethal 4800-mile range Submarine-Launched Ballistic Missiles (SLBMs) over the Artic at targets which included Washington, DC and any others within an arc drawn from South Carolina through Oklahoma to Oregon. It was for this very reason that President Ronald Reagan's Secretary of the Navy, John F Lehman, became fond of describing Murmansk and the rest of the Kola Peninsula as 'the most valuable piece of real estate on earth'.

But surveillance of the ports from where these powerful submarines would sail was particularly difficult even for satellites due to the prevailing weather conditions which, for the most part, consisted of persistent cloud cover, rain, fog and, of course, the long, dark Artic winters. Even on clear days, the sun angle in the Barents Sea was often too low for the collection of high-resolution photography due to high reflectivity.

In May 1978, mindful of the SR-71's HRR Radar Intelligence (RadInt) gathering capabilities, Adm Holloway requested that the Defense Intelligence Agency (DIA) validate such a mission requirement over Murmansk and the Kola Peninsula. The DIA's evaluation indicated that seven such flights per month would be required to fulfil the US Navy's requirement, but it concluded that the SR-71 should first fly three evaluation sorties.

In 1978 the number of Primary Authorised Aircraft (jets for which funds were available to operate) available to the 9th SRW stood at just eight SR-71s. With commitments in the Western Pacific, to the SIOP, the

Until work began on the construction of a pair of bespoke 'barns' in 1985, Mildenhall-based SR-71s utilised a less than ideal hangar complex on the airfield's south side (*Paul F Crickmore*)

Strategic Projection Force, two or three annual deployments to Mildenhall and training operations at Beale, it was rightly thought that the level of coverage required by the CNO was well beyond what was possible with the assets then available, so the matter was put on hold.

On 16 October 1978, 64-17964 returned to Mildenhall, being ferried in by Majs Rich Graham and Don Emmons – the 9th SRW's Standards and Evaluation crew. The jet stayed for 16 days, and Maj B C Thomas and his RSO Maj Jay Reid took turns with the 'Stan/Eval' crew to collect RadInt and ELINT of the Soviet troop rotation, but neither ventured into the Barents Sea. Instead Kadena-based SR-71s collected RadInt of the Soviet Pacific Fleet, based around Vladivostok, for the CNO.

YEMEN

In early 1979, the established cycle of SR-71 deployments to Mildenhall during the spring and autumn to participate in NATO exercises and monitor the Soviet/Warsaw Pact troop rotations was interrupted by the threat of yet another war in the Middle East.

Situated on the tip of the Arabian Peninsula and at the southern approach to the Red Sea, North and South Yemen bordered oil-rich Saudi Arabia. One of the few Arab nations still friendly to the United States, Saudi Arabia was its largest foreign supplier of oil. Throughout the 1970s South Yemen had received military aid from both China and the Soviet Union. In addition, it had repeatedly tried to undermine the more moderate government of North Yemen. Saudi Arabia had close ties with the latter country, but not with the left wing government to the south. On 24 February 1979, whilst the foreign minister from South Yemen was in Riyadh, pledging that his government would support Arab League arbitration over the problems that existed between the north and south, his government ordered the invasion of their northern neighbour.

This action caused considerable consternation within the Saudi royal family, who feared that a united Yemen under a Marxist government would infiltrate their country and destabilise it politically. So, in response to a Saudi request made through the DIA, the JCS directed HQ SAC to deploy an SR-71 to Mildenhall on 12 March 1979 – one month before the due date to cover the spring Warsaw Pact troop rotation. The 9th SRW had been tasked with conducting a single *Giant Reach* special mission into the Middle East in order to secure surveillance relating to events that had developed in this latest hot spot.

Despite a 3 March ceasefire that had supposedly come into effect between North and South Yemen, intelligence sources advised the DIA that fighting was continuing, particularly in the regions of Qatabah and Harib. As a result of this news, the JCS's earlier decision to deploy on 12 March remained in effect.

One of two crews to cover the deployment consisted of Majs 'Buzz' Carpenter and John Murphy, and the former now takes up the story from Sunday, 11 March – the day before the scheduled departure from Beale;

'John and I looked over the mission paths, as the package called for three sorties to be flown into the Middle East two to three days apart from Mildenhall. We knew our preferred routes into the Middle East from the UK, but once again the French refused to let the SR-71 fly through their airspace for quick access into the Mediterranean Sea – heading across

France would have reduced the duration of this almost ten-hour mission by two-and-a-half hours and one air refuelling.

'Other questions focused on looking for suitable bases for our tankers. The special JP-7 fuel was stored at Mildenhall, Incirlik and Moron air base, near Seville in Spain. Turkey and Israel said the tankers would not be allowed to operate from their airfields, and Saudi Arabia was not chosen either. Finally, Cairo West air base in Egypt was selected, and the tankers would have to transport the JP-7 there from Turkey, as they could not directly support us from Incirlik.

'As one can imagine, the most critical aspect for us when it came to working out mission timings was for the tanker crews to determine their best basing sites and then get the KC-135Qs, their aircrews and their maintenance support personnel into those locations. The SR-71 might be able to fly at Mach 3+ at high altitude, but without the tankers operating from their forward-deployed locations, the "Habu" was simply not mission-capable.

'John and I were told that we would be part of the advanced party heading to Mildenhall to receive the SR-71 deploying from Beale, which was being flown in by one of our most experienced and senior crews, Majs Rich Graham and Don Emmons. We took a quick trip home, picked up our bags and said goodbye to our families – we didn't know when we'd be back – then stopped by the squadron to pick-up our checklists and various deployment materials. We had to secure a special UHF radio and other items to be used by the mobile crew to launch and recover the SR-71 from our deployment base at Mildenhall.

'A last minute delay meant that our tanker didn't depart Beale until nearly 1800 hrs. Time would be really tight now. We flew to Pease AFB, New Hampshire, at the KC-135's top speed. A scheduled quick refuelling at Pease was a must, so the tanker crew called ahead and tried to ensure that everything would be ready to go for our high-priority mission. Fortunately, everything went according to plan, with fuel trucks standing by to refuel the aircraft and box lunches on hand for the tanker aircrew and all of us passengers. John and I went into base operations and made a few essential telephone calls to update the overall mission status, determine a revised arrival time for the SR-71 into Mildenhall and receive further instructions. We then rushed back to the tanker, and shortly afterwards we were back in the air heading across the North Atlantic.

'Upon landing at Mildenhall, we had at most just 30 minutes before the SR-71 touched-down. We leapt into the Mobile car, hot-wired the special radio into its electrical system, mounted its external antenna and proceeded immediately towards the runway to complete our recovery checklists. The latter included gaining clearance from the tower to access the runway and carry out a visible inspection for any possible Foreign Object Damage items that could puncture the SR-71's tyres.

'As we were checking the runway for screws, bolts etc., John made contact with Rich and Don – affectionately known as "Snake" and "Nape". They were ten minutes out and about to go over to approach control for recovery. We then played about a minute of "Darl'n" (a David Allen Coe song that had almost become the theme song for the SR-71 programme at this point in time) over the radio. It was late in the afternoon as '972, using the call sign "Awry 26", touched down.

'Tankers were still getting into position, and the mission planning team with us worked into the night finalising the three mission objective routes over the Arabian Peninsula, focusing on the Saudi-Yemeni border. Refuelling tracks had by now been established, with the first off Land's End, the second over the Mediterranean Sea, a third over the Red Sea going in and a fourth again over the Red Sea coming out. The final refuelling would be a long drag over the central Mediterranean, abeam Libya, to get us home. Because we were banned from flying over France, the last leg would be a critical one for fuel.

'By Tuesday afternoon the tankers were in place, and if the weather permitted we would launch the first mission Wednesday morning (14 March). Early departure was required to place the SR-71 over the Arabian Peninsula with optimum daylight for the cameras. We met at 1500 hrs on Tuesday for a briefing, and there were representatives from many organisations that we did not normally see. This attested to the importance of the mission. We had attaches from our embassy, senior National Security Agency reps, the "two star" USAF Director of Operations from SAC and many others. The "two star" had questions about our operations, being "interested in the route we were about to fly, potential divert bases and the rules of engagement we were given to operate within".'

To ensure that they got adequate rest, the SR-71 crews retired to bed at 1800 hrs. They would be woken at 0100 hrs for a physical examination, eat a high protein, low residue breakfast of steak and eggs and then be kitted out in their pressure suits and driven to the aircraft. Meanwhile, Majs Rich Graham and Don Emmons would conduct a pre-flight inspection of the 'Habu' so that all would be ready for the scheduled 0400 hrs engine start. With everything 'good to go' as planned, the weather in the target area intervened and the mission was placed on hold for 24 hours. Unfortunately, weather again delayed the operation at 0400 hrs on Thursday.

Enjoying an early seafood dinner at the Mildenhall Officers' Club that evening, Majs Carpenter and Murphy again retired, hopeful that the following day's weather would at last enable them to perform their important mission. Maj Carpenter continues his story;

'At last we were off on this adventure. Everything went as per the schedule and we blasted off into the night at 0430 hrs, heading across England at 25,000 ft towards the southwest and our tankers near Land's End. This was quite a change for us, as we normally headed east out over the North Sea and hooked up with our tankers fairly quickly. As we flew west I seemed to have more intestinal gas than normal. I figured that it would pass as we climbed and the cabin pressure rose to 28,000 ft. It was very common for us to work on relieving our gas build up as we climbed.

'It took almost 30 minutes before we were hooked up with the first of our tankers. By now I was feeling really uncomfortable. John and I discussed our options. We couldn't proceed if I was sick, but I did not want the mission scrubbed and have it reported to the National Security Council (NSC) that after two nights of slippage the operation was again postponed because the pilot was sick! On the second tanker I had a quick diarrhoea attack (the "seafood special" we figured), but afterwards I felt much better. Then came the next question – was there any adverse effect from "sitting on this stuff" for the next nine hours?! John and I discussed this with the tanker crew, and I felt that I was fine to proceed.

Prior to launch, the pilot would line the aircraft on the runway centreline, whereupon its wheels were chocked (as seen here at Mildenhall). The pilot would then increase power one engine at a time and fine-tune the exhaust gas temperature (EGT), before engaging the automatic engine trim to ensure maximum engine efficiency on take-off (*Paul F Crickmore*)

A typical view from the cockpit of an SR-71 cruising at speed and altitude – the curvature of the earth is not too well defined because water molecules in the troposphere often create a layer of haze. But as the Sun goes up or down through the terminator (the line dividing the illuminated and dark part of the planet), it is possible to see the curvature – it is accentuated here by a wide-angle lens (*B C Thomas*)

'We dropped off the tanker over the Atlantic Ocean, and with a full load of fuel began our climb and acceleration whilst heading due south. The sun had by then come up, and we arrived at our cruising altitude of 74,000 ft at Mach 3.0. A turn east was executed, taking us through the Straits of Gibraltar and into the Mediterranean. By now I felt pretty good, and we set up to initiate our descent and deceleration for our second refuelling. All proceeded as normal with the tankers from Spain, and they were glad to see us at last after a third day of flying in support of this mission. As directed, at the end of the refuelling we called "operationally normal" over the radio and started our next acceleration and climb. So far there has been no reaction from any potentially hostile areas.

'Now departing the Mediterranean, the view of the Pyramids and the Sphinx was spectacular! It was time to start down once more. John said that we were not getting the normal ranging information from the tankers to adjust our rendezvous profile. Unbeknownst to us, the tanker radios were not working, and they actually saw our contrails as we started down. Through past experience, they set-up their turns to roll out in front of us at the right spacing and speed. This was outstanding teamwork, and typical of the "can-do" attitude that made it all happen within the 9th SRW.

'The refuelling went without a hitch, but we were unaware that two Egyptian MiG-23s had followed our tankers out on this third day to see "what was going on". Unknown to us, a picture was taken from the second tanker, which was above us, as we refuelled. Months later, John and I signed a copy of the photo, which was then presented to the Egyptian Embassy and Egyptian Air Force to thank them for their great support. The picture was wonderful, showing three tankers in formation, us refuelling under the second tanker and the pair of MiGs about 200-300 yards in trail.

'With full tanks, we were now off for acceleration and climb number three, but this one would take us into our objective area. Defensive systems were again checked, and all other aircraft systems were functioning normally. Aircraft "972" was performing exceedingly well.

'As we passed through 45,000 ft at Mach 2.4 we got a fighter attack radar indication coming from our right forward quadrant. We determined that a Middle Eastern fighter would not be a threat to us at this speed and altitude – after returning to California, I talked with Kelly Johnson about this event, as he'd been cleared into any of the missions and occurrences we might see or experience. I turned left as we reached Mach 3.0 at 75,000 ft. What a view – sand for as far as I could see, with the occasional interspersed oasis. It was incredible to think that they were fighting over control of this open desert. There was sand blowing around below us, making for a hazy scene. Above, the sky was as black as ever.

'As we flew over the Yemeni-Saudi border area, I prepared to make a left turn for a second loop over this objective. Hardly a word was spoken between John and I during these intense, high-activity time periods. Just as everything seemed to be working as planned, the aircraft tried to make a right instead of the planned left turn. I disconnected the autopilot and got us turning left. John was working to see if he could locate the source of the problem, as well as checking the rest of the objective area to ensure that we had maintained route integrity. We were on that mythical black line, swinging through for another pass.

'As we left the objective area, we were in a right descending, decelerating turn, looking for our fourth set of tankers. We were a little low on fuel by this time because of the extra manoeuvring, but again the refuelling went without a hitch. Once off the tankers, we climbed for the return leg to the UK. After this extended cruising leg, we started our last refuelling – number five. This one would be different from the rest as a normal refuelling lasted 15-20 minutes and transferred 80,000+ lbs of fuel. The goal was to reach your end ARCP with full tanks, ready to begin your acceleration. However, for this last refuelling we'd stay behind the tanker for 50 minutes, dragging along subsonically to give us a closer end ARCP. This would ensure that we had the extra fuel needed on board to deal with the potentially bad British weather. The refuelling was carried out in the middle of the Mediterranean, north of Libya. Everyone was closely monitoring radar traffic to see if Libya detected and then reacted to our presence.

'Descent and hook-up went flawlessly. I thought about dropping off the tanker a couple of times and re-engaging to top off the fuel in the aircraft, but the decision was made that instead of risking not being able to hook-up again, the easiest action was to stay on the second tanker's boom for about 45 minutes. We saw a lot of air traffic over the Mediterranean during this time, but none of it is out of the ordinary.

'With our tanks topped off, John and I were ready for the last leg. We had been in our pressure suits now for more than nine hours, and I'd later learn that with the normal dehydrating 100 per cent oxygen breathing environment in the cockpit, coupled with my earlier illness, I'd lost more than eight pounds in weight, even though I had been eating tube food and drinking water throughout the mission.

'Climb and acceleration were normal, and we passed back through the Straits of Gibraltar and started a turn to the north, heading home. Prior to our descent, we learned that it was raining at Mildenhall. The descent took us down in such a way that we entered the UK landmass subsonically. Driving across the country under radar approach control, we set up for a precision landing. However, while running through the recovery checklist we determined that the nose gear did not want to come down. Now in the rain, we would have to run the alternate gear-lowering checklist, which meant leaving the landing gear selection handle down, pulling some circuit breakers and then releasing a cable in the front cockpit. Whilst going through these actions, we terminated the precision approach and switched to a visual approach instead. After what seemed liked an eternity, the gear dropped into the down and locked position.

'We fooled the "birdwatchers" on this occasion, as there were very few around the airfield to watch our return to Mildenhall in the rain at the end of our ten-hour mission. Landing, thankfully, was uneventful, and as we taxied into our parking position outside the hangar it seemed that all the deployment personnel were standing around cheering our mission completion. John and I felt so honoured to be a part of this great team. Engine shutdown commenced and the gantry stand was rolled up beside us. I felt pretty good, but a little weak. I tried to tactfully tell the groundcrew not to get too close, and there was a pervading odour.

'Unbeknownst to John and I, the first tanker had relayed our problem back to base, and during the flight the team had organised a little ceremony. At the foot of the ladder the 9th SRW's vice wing commander, Col Dave Young, met me to get a quick debrief, but more importantly to present me with an SR-71 tie tack that they had painted brown. Its accompanying certificate attested that on this date I was the first "surely not true, but funny" supersonic turd. What could I say! Laughter came from everywhere. I felt okay, so the PSD guys gave me my customary after-flight beer – re-hydration was also a critical part of this high flight.

'As it turned out, our mission would be the only one flown by the SR-71 over the Middle East during this particular crisis. All the data required by the NSC had been collected, meeting Presidential needs. On 28 March, John and I launched "Snake" and "Nape" into the air as "Input 62", taking "972" home. To this day, Rich still kids me about tricking him into having the Chief of Standardization Aircrew for the 9th SRW act as a "mere" ferry crew for us. Such is the luck of life.'

A surprisingly large number of colourful artworks and badges were applied to various SR-71s over the years. From 24 October to 16 November 1977, 64-17976 displayed large 9th SRW badges on its fins while detached to Mildenhall (*Lindsay Peacock*)

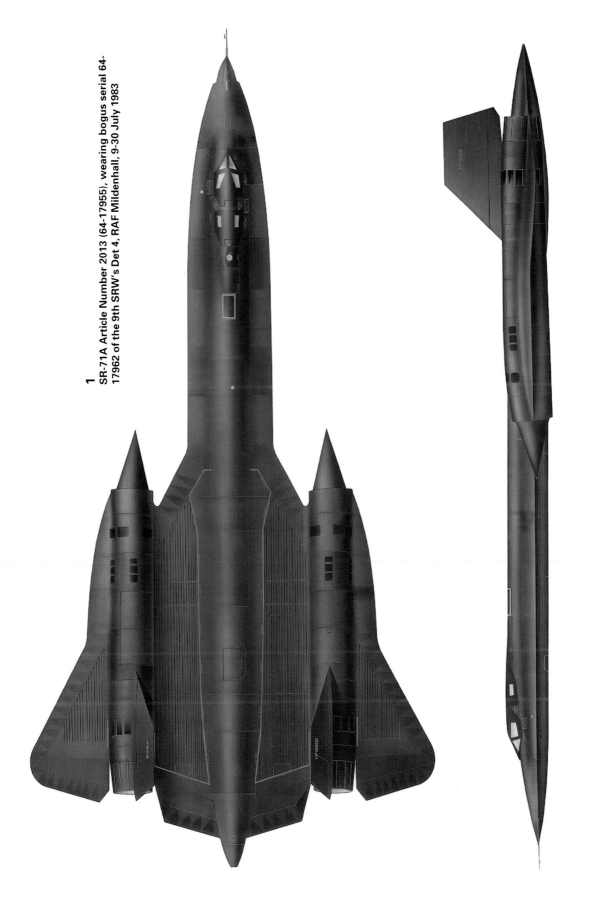

1
SR-71A Article Number 2013 (64-17955), wearing bogus serial 64-17962 of the 9th SRW's Det 4, RAF Mildenhall, 9-30 July 1983

2
SR-71C Article Number 2000 (64-17981) of the 9th SRW, Beale AFB, March 1969 to April 1976

3
SR-71A Article Number 2006 (64-17955), Air Force Logistics Command, Palmdale, August 1965 to January 1985

4
SR-71A Article Number 2027 (64-17976) of the 9th SRW, RAF Mildenhall, 24 October to 16 November 1977

5
SR-71B Article Number 2007 (64-17956), 9th SRW, Beale AFB, 1965 to 1990

6
SR-71A Article Number 2015 (64-17964) of the 9th SRW's Det 4, RAF Mildenhall 16 August to 6 November 1981

7
SR-71A Article Number 2010 (64-17959) of Det 51, Palmdale, 20 November 1975 to 24 October 1976

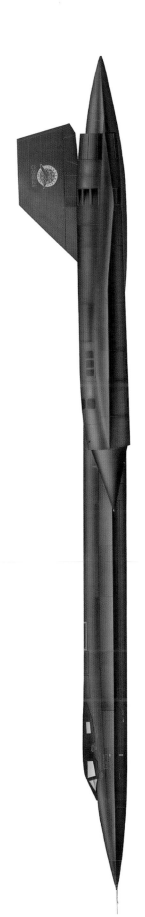

8 SR-71A Article Number 2031 (64-17980), 9th SRW, Beale AFB, 1990

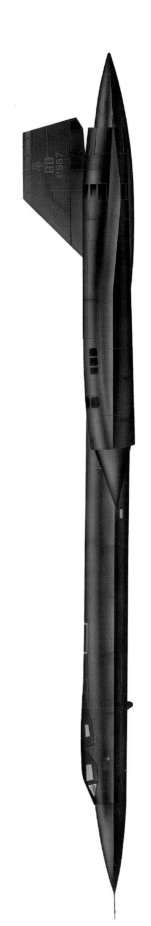

9
SR-71A Article Number 2031 (64-17980), NASA, Edwards AFB, September 1992 to October 1999

10
SR-71A Article Number 2018 (64-17967) of the 9th SRW's Det 2, Beale AFB, October 1997

3

4

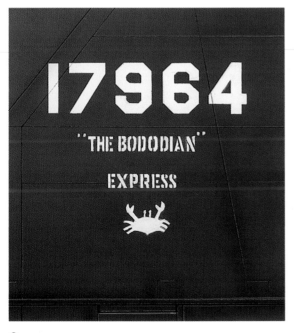

6

8

DETACHMENT 4 IS FORMED

The success of the Yemen mission, and the various exercise deployments in the years preceding it, convinced the USAF that the 9th SRW should have a more permanent presence at RAF Mildenhall. Thus, on 31 March 1979, Detachment 4 was created as the European SR-71 and TR-1 operating unit. Its first task was to provide surveillance of the Soviet spring troop rotation, with missions being flown by Majs Bill Groninger and Lee Shelton, together with their respective RSOs, Majs Chuck Sober and Barry MacKean. Aircraft 64-17979 was tasked with performing these sorties, the jet arriving at Mildenhall as 'Fern 29' on 17 April and departing on 2 May.

In response to the CNO's requests for RadInt of the Barents Sea, the very first round-robin mission into the region was flown from Beale on 13 July 1979 in support of SAC worldwide nuclear readiness exercise *Global Shield 79*. The 10 hour 4 minute mission obtained HRR imagery of the targeted area, and two similar missions were conducted in 1980.

The autumn troop rotation of 1979 was covered from 18 October to 13 November by Majs Rich Young and RSO Russ Szczepanik and Majs Joe Kinego and RSO Bill Keller in 64-17976. The same aircraft returned for the 1980 spring rotation on 9 April, and three 'Habu' crews flew it during the 30-day deployment. 64-17972 arrived as 'Cup 10' and covered the autumn rotation between 13 September and 2 November, four crews sharing the mission load. However, due to the resurfacing of Mildenhall's runway, the jet was flown into nearby RAF Lakenheath, from where it continued to operate until returning to Beale as 'Room 60'.

On 12 December 1980, a third SR-71 deployment to Mildenhall occurred. This time the JCS had directed that Det 4 should conduct a series of missions in response to a request from the US Commander in Chief Atlantic Command (USCinCACOM), who was concerned at the possible intervention of Soviet military forces to quell rising dissent in Poland. Majs Rich Young and RSO Russ Szczepanik duly arrived in

On 31 March 1979, Det 4 of the 9th SRW was established at RAF Mildenhall. As its first unit badge clearly shows, at this stage Det 4 was a joint SR-71/TR-1 operator (*Bob Archer*)

The Warsaw Pact spring troop rotation of 1979 was monitored by SR-71 64-17979. Note the 9th SRW emblem on the aircraft's tail (*Bob Archer*)

64-17964, having collected an HRR/ELINT take on their inbound leg to Mildenhall. This was to prove a milestone deployment, with the aircraft staying in the UK for four months until it was replaced by 64-17972 the day prior to its return to Beale on 6 March. The latter SR-71 stayed for two months, before eventually departing for Beale on 5 May 1981 as 'Yappy 22'.

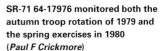

Not all round-robins went as planned, however. For example, the mission scheduled for 12 August 1981 was meant to see SR-71 64-17964 take off from Beale, overfly the Barents Sea and then return to its

SR-71 64-17976 monitored both the autumn troop rotation of 1979 and the spring exercises in 1980 (*Paul F Crickmore*)

California home. Majs B C Thomas and RSO Jay Reid duly took off at 2200 hrs to fly the ten-and-a-half-hour sortie, with refuellings over Idaho, Goose Bay, twice over the North Sea and again over Goose Bay, before returning to Beale. Between the two North Sea refuellings they would make a run over the Barents Sea, where their side-looking HRR would pick-up Soviet submarine targets for the US Navy.

The mission went like clockwork until they were in the 'take' area, at which point Maj Thomas noticed

that his left engine low 'oil-quantity' warning light was flashing on and off. After completing the important radar run, he commenced refuelling from one of the KC-135Qs. Whilst on the tanker Thomas noted that the oil warning light was now on continuously. This was a 'mandatory abort' item on his emergency procedures checklist because prolonged flight under such degraded conditions could easily result in engine seizure. There were two preferred bases in northwest Europe for diversionary aborts – Mildenhall, which would take two-and-a-half hours to reach at subsonic speeds, or Bødo, in Norway, which was just 20 minutes away.

Thomas decided that caution was the better part of valour on this

Majs B C Thomas and Jay Reid became the first crew to land an SR-71 at a Continental European air base when, on 12 August 1981, they diverted 64-17964 into Bødo, Norway (*B C Thomas*)

Maj B C Thomas took this self-portrait during a Det 4 flight. He accrued 1217 hours and 18 minutes in th SR-71 – more than any other 'Habu' pilot (*B C Thomas*)

occasion and diverted into Bødo. Once there he was greeted by the base commander, Gen Ohmount of the Royal Norwegian Air Force (RNAF), who, as Thomas recalled, was very polite but very nervous. It later transpired that Ohmount had been a young lieutenant at the base in 1960 when Gary Powers had been shot down. After it became widely known that the intention was for the CIA pilot to have landed at Bødo, the Norwegian government disclaimed

64-17964 appeared again at Mildenhall on 16 August 1981, but this was an unscheduled visit following its earlier diversion into Bødo with an engine oil warning – a mandatory abort item on the emergency procedures checklist. As a result the jet had the words *"THE BODONIAN" Express* painted onto its twin tail fins (*Paul F Crickmore*)

The international airspace over the Barents and Baltic Seas were extremely important intelligence gathering areas for Det 4 SR-71s. Here 64-17964 formates on the right wing of a KC-135Q in the 'Viking North' air refuelling track (probably one of the USAF's most northerly air refuelling areas). Note condensation trails from two other 'Q birds' in the track (*Paul F Crickmore*)

any knowledge of the plan and fired Ohmount's boss at that time – an event that was still strongly etched on his memory!

Having notified the SAC SRC of his intentions to divert, Thomas was anxious to provide 'home plate' with other details. The Norwegian general directed the 'Habu' pilot towards his underground command post – a very impressive facility built into the side of a mountain – from where Thomas could tell Col Dave Young (CO of the 9th SRW) of the nature of 64-17964's mechanical problem. Young asked at what stage the decision had been made to abort, to which Thomas gave the total mission time and the third air refuelling time. From that answer, Col Young was able to ascertain that the aircraft had the reconnaissance 'take' on board, and that certain specialists would need to accompany the recovery crew to download the data.

An RNAF officer was then assigned to each of the 'Habu' aircrew – Thomas recalled that his 'minder' was F-104 pilot Lt Roar Strand of the 331st Fighter Squadron. The Norwegian pilots did not let their charges out of their sight, and even slept in the same rooms. The recovery team, headed up by Lt Col Randy Hertzog, arrived in a KC-135Q on 15 August. Gen Ohmount had requested that the team wear military uniforms and not civilian clothes to ensure that all was kept 'above board'. Unfortunately, this message didn't reach the new arrivals, who were quickly ushered back onto the tanker and instructed to don their fatigues.

With a million members of the Polish Solidarity movement having gone on strike on 7 August, and mounting tension between communist state officials and the rest of the Polish population, it was decided that 64-17964 should remain in Europe to monitor any possible Soviet response. Consequently, at 1342 hrs on 16 August, Thomas and Reid departed Bødo in the company of their trusty tanker for a return flight to Mildenhall, which was performed at subsonic speed. Bearing the inscription *"THE BØDONIAN" EXPRESS* on its twin tails, 64-17964 touched down at 1452 hrs. The crew was met at the bottom of the gantry platform by two other 'Habu' crew members, Majs Jerry Glasser and RSO Mac Hornbaker, who would fly the next 'Bødonian Express' sortie into the Baltic and along the coast of Poland on 22 August.

A week later, Thomas and Reid performed a third sortie to the same area, and this was followed up by Capts Rich Young and Ed Bethart on 31 August. Finally, on 2 September Thomas and Reid returned to Beale by tanker. Their scheduled ten-hour sortie had lasted 21 days! 64-17964 continued to operate from Mildenhall until 6 November, when it too returned to Beale.

The political situation in Poland continued to deteriorate as the clamour for reforms and democracy gathered momentum. By early December things had reached breaking point, and on the night of the 12th Poland's communist leader, Gen Wojciech Jaruzelski, cut all communication links with the West and deployed troops and armour to set up roadblocks and occupy strategic installations. He then declared a state of martial law and appeared on television to announce the formation of a Military Council of National Salvation. He claimed that strikes, protest demonstrations and crime had brought the country 'to the border of mental endurance and the verge of an abyss'.

Two days later it became apparent that at least 14,000 trade union activists had been rounded up and arrested and seven had been shot in the Silesian coal fields while resisting martial law. Would Gen Jaruzelski turn to the Soviet Union for help in his struggle to retain control of Poland, or would President Leonid Brezhnev commit Soviet troops to crush the uprising, as he had done in Czechoslovakia on 21 August 1968? Clearly, the Reagan Administration needed some answers, and fast, and as ever the SR-71 and its crews were on hand to provide them.

Capts Gil Bertelson and RSO Frank Stampf were on the roster for this important sortie. The significance of their mission dictated that it was to be backed up by a spare aircraft. Consequently, Majs Nevin Cunningham and RSO Geno Quist (known within the crew force as 'Neno' and 'Geno') were also suited-up as 'spares'. As Bertelson and Stampf departed Beale and disappeared with their SR-71 into the cold, wet, night, Cunningham and Quist waited at the end of the runway in 64-17958 for the code words that would either send them 'back to the barn' or on their way over much of the North Atlantic and northern Europe. Soon after, Stampf called back to Quist on their discrete HF radio frequency, saying simply 'Your guys have got it', to which both spare crewmen simultaneously said 'Oh Shit', and off they went.

The weather in the first air refuelling area over Nevada and Utah was so bad that it was all the 'Habu' crew could do to find the tanker in the thick clouds. When they finally located it, and were 'on the boom', it proved extremely difficult for Cunningham to

Majs B C Thomas and Jay Reid taxi 64-17964 to Det 4's operating area after landing at Mildenhall following their flight from Bødo on 16 August 1981. Note *"THE BODONIAN" Express* titling freshly applied to the jet's twin fins in Norway (*Lindsay Peacock*)

64-17964's return to Det 4 in August 1981 had been totally unscheduled, as the jet had only recently spent three months at Mildenhall from 12 December 1980 through to 7 March 1981. SAC was ordered by the JCS to keep the jet with Det 4 (which had no SR-71 assigned to it at the time) until 6 November 1981 due to the growing political crisis in Poland (*Paul F Crickmore*)

maintain the connection due to heavy turbulence. The updrafts bounced the KC-135 all over the sky to the degree that its autopilot was unable to react fast enough to the unstable conditions. As a result, this refuelling proved to be one of the most difficult experienced by both the tanker and SR-71 crews involved. Cunningham asked the KC-135 pilot to forget autopilot and 'go manual' to achieve a better 'offload platform'. Meanwhile, the transfer operation was enshrouded in Saint Elmo's Fire, which lit up both aircraft like glowing Christmas trees.

After completing the ragged refuelling, Cunningham lit both 'burners and pressed on to the second ARCP over Canada. Once again the weather did its utmost to make the operation as uncomfortable as possible. After crossing the Atlantic, they headed for their third refuelling track off the west coast of Norway. Here, they were sandwiched between layers of cloud, but the air was smooth in the Arctic twilight and the top-off went smoothly.

The long Atlantic crossing required a split off-load from two tankers, and after taking half of the fuel from one KC-135, Cunningham looked for the second tanker. As he closed in on the aircraft, he discovered that he was actually joining up with a Soviet Ilyushin Il-20 'Coot' ELINT aircraft! Cunningham flew 64-17958 up to the 'would-be' tanker, who was no doubt just as startled by the presence of a 'Habu'. The crew quickly dropped back to find the second tanker, and after taking on more fuel, the pilot lit the 'burners for the next high-hot run.

At 72,000 ft, Cunningham and Quist headed into the 'take' area, where it was especially dark at altitude. Indeed, it seemed that the only source of light was coming from the SR-71's afterburners 100 ft behind them. Having completed an inner 'loop' around the Baltic Sea, they were on their way back down to the fourth refuelling track when the sun popped back up over the horizon.

To further complicate matters on this long and difficult mission, Quist was unable to make radio contact with the tankers. Fortunately, Cunningham spotted contrails well below and ahead of them, and simply followed the aerial 'railroad tracks' for a join up. While on the boom, Quist broke further bad news to his pilot about their Astro-Inertial Navigation System (ANS), which had failed. Clearly it would not be possible to return to Beale, since 'ANS Failure' was a mandatory abort item. The crew therefore settled into formation with the tankers, who led them to Mildenhall, where snow and ice covered the runway and taxiways. Finally, after what had turned out to be a 'very entertaining' mission, 64-17958 slithered to a halt outside the dedicated SR-71 barn and Cunningham and Quist climbed out after their eight-and-a-half hour 'fun filled' mission – their 27th sortie together.

On 6 October 1981, Maj Rich Judson and RSO Lt Col Frank Kelly flew 64-17964 on a Barents/Baltic Seas sortie. It is seen here during the course of the mission in the 'Viking North' air refuelling track (*Paul F Crickmore*)

Maj Nevin Cunningham (left), who was no stranger to Mildenhall, later became Det 4's CO. He is seen here talking to Lt Col Joe Kinego, who was CO of the 1st Strategic Reconnaissance Squadron at the time this photograph was taken (*Paul F Crickmore*)

Back at Beale, the Californian winter weather was less severe, and as Majs B C Thomas and Jay Reid deplaned from a 9th SRW T-38 following the completion of a routine training flight on 16 December, they were met by wing deputy CO, Col Randy Hertzog. He instructed them to go home and grab whatever they needed for an indefinite deployment to Mildenhall. The KC-135 carrying both them and a maintenance team departed Beale at 1930 hrs and arrived in England at 0730 hrs the following morning.

On 18 December Majs Cunningham and Quist flew 64-17958 on a second sortie over the Baltic, and another mission that would end at Beale was planned for Thomas and Reid as soon as they were crew-rested from their transatlantic flight. An analysis of Quist's 'take' had revealed that the Soviet Union was not making preparations to intervene militarily to quell Poland's political unrest.

Thomas and Reid departed Mildenhall in 64-17958 on 21 December and headed out over the North Sea for the first of five aerial refuellings. They too had been tasked with monitoring the Soviet/Polish border situation from a stand-off position in international airspace over the Baltic Sea. Their mission profile also included a lengthy run around the coast of Norway and up along the northern coast of the USSR. Reid activated the sensors as they cruised at Mach 3 on their northern loop, which saw the jet exit the 'take' area near Murmansk on a westerly heading, bound for its fourth refuelling. Out over the North Atlantic, the right generator cut off, but Thomas managed to get it reset.

After the fifth tanking near Goose Bay, Labrador, another problem arose that would limit their cruise speed inbound to Beale. During acceleration, Thomas noted that 64-17958's supply of liquid nitrogen had been depleted, and that the fuel tanks could not be pressurised to inert the fuel fumes at high Mach. He limited the cruise Mach to 2.6 in accordance with emergency operating procedures, and made his final descent into Beale lower on fuel after a flight of almost ten hours.

This series of Baltic sorties had not only obtained invaluable intelligence for the Reagan Administration at a time of high international tension, they had also vividly demonstrated US resolve to stay actively engaged in the situation by using its key surveillance assets in the NATO-Warsaw Pact theatre of operations.

Det 4's capability was doubled during 1982 when two SR-71s were based 'permanently' at Mildenhall for the first

Dependent upon weight, ambient air temperature and pressure, normal approach speed for an SR-71 when landing at Mildenhall was 175 knots, with ten degrees of nose-up pitch. Final flare further increased the angle of the nose-up pitch, thus reducing speed to 155 knots for touch down (*Paul F Crickmore*)

Aside from crew fatigue, the ultimate limiting factor on SR-71 mission endurance was the jet's nitrogen capacity. Gaseous nitrogen was used to pressurise both the TEB and the fuel tanks as they became depleted, otherwise the part-occupied tanks would have been crushed by the increasing atmospheric pressure as the aircraft descended to cruise altitudes (*Lockheed*)

49

time. The aircraft, manned by crews on 30-day deployments, flew a succession of 'routine, but highly productive, missions' across the North Sea and Eastern Europe. 64-17972 was one of the two jets operated during this period, and following seven months on deployment, it was ready to be returned to Beale for periodic heavy maintenance. The latter included the replacement of fuel tank sealant that tended to burn away after repeated high-Mach flights. Majs Cunningham and Quist got the big redeployment sortie, and they left Mildenhall at 1000 hrs on 5 July 1983 and headed for the Barents/Baltic Seas, prior to flying west across the North Atlantic and back to California.

After completing their first 'take' run on a 'northern loop' over the Barents Sea, the crew decelerated into the 'Viking North' aerial refuelling track in international airspace west of Bodø. Topped off, they climbed back to altitude and entered their second 'collection area' within the narrow Baltic corridor to complete the reconnaissance portion of the mission. Preparing to head home, they again decelerated and descended into the 'Viking North' area over the North Sea. Back at high altitude after taking on more fuel, Quist calculated that Cunningham would have to accelerate to maximum Mach to improve the aircraft's range so as to ensure that they would have enough fuel to reach the next set of tankers near Labrador.

During this 'high and hot' phase of the flight, the SR-71's left engine's EGT indicator showed that the temperature of the exhaust gas exiting the J58 had become uncontrollable, and that 64-17972 should not be flown faster than Mach 3.05 in order to prevent the powerplant being damaged. However, by flying at this less than optimum speed the SR-71 would run out of fuel before it reached the KC-135s. Manual control of the

64-17974 arrived in England on 30 April 1982 for an eight-month stint with Det 4 (*Lindsay Peacock*)

Below
64-17980 deployed to Det 4 from 5 January through 27 April 1982, when it was replaced by 64-17974. The mid-semi-span position of the engines are immediately apparent from this shot, taken by a No 41 Sqn Jaguar during a sortie from RAF Coltishall (*Crown Copyright*)

Bottom
64-17974 set the record deployment time to date when it left Det 4 on 13 December 1982 (*Paul F Crickmore*)

64-17971 arrived at Mildenhall on 23 December 1982, and with 64-17972 having already flown in just five days earlier, it meant that for the first time in its history Det 4 had two SR-71s under its command (*Lindsay Peacock*)

inlet spikes and doors made fuel consumption even worse, and the crew was only able to maintain Mach 3 in this configuration. Slowing to subsonic speeds would further exacerbate their low fuel predicament, and they found that they were beyond the point of no return to go back to Bødo. Therefore, Cunningham and Quist had no choice but to press on toward their KC-135Qs in the hope that they might be able to improve their fuel flow rate or divert into Iceland. For the next 45 minutes Cunningham flew at Mach 3.09, before slowing to 3.05 to allow the EGT to drop back into the 'green'.

As they approached the 'point-of-no-return' off Iceland, Quist recalculated the fuel situation, which had improved slightly. Once availed of this news, Cunningham decided to press on, and he told his RSO to get the tankers to fly toward them so as to speed up the refuelling rendezvous. After completing a hook-up in record-breaking time, the fuel streamed into 64-17972 at more than 6000 lbs per minute. Once back at Beale after another seven hours of SR-71 excitement, neither crewmember would admit to how much (or how little) fuel they had remaining before they made contact with their everlasting friends in the tanker.

64-17955

In May 1983 HQ SAC and AFSC decided to test the effectiveness of Goodyear's Advanced Synthetic Aperture Radar System-1 (ASARS-1) on an SR-71 prior to upgrading the rest of the 'Habu' fleet with this new high-definition, ground-mapping equipment. 64-17955 was duly equipped with the system, and Majs B C Thomas and RSO John Morgan were assigned the task of conducting the first operational test flight with the equipment fitted.

Captured on 'finals', '64-17962', flown by Majs Maury Rosenberg and RSO E D McKim, prepares to land at Mildenhall on 9 July 1983, having completed an operational sortie into the Barents/Baltic Seas collection area. In fact, false serial numbers had been applied to the aircraft specially for its three-week deployment with Det 4, as this airframe was in fact 64-17955 (*Bob Archer*)

On 1 July 1983, they carried out SAC's first ASARS-1 familiarisation flight, which lasted just over five hours. During the mission Morgan got to grips with the ASARS-1 'switchology' and the system's operating techniques. Five days later, Majs Maury Rosenberg and RSO E D McKim also flew 64-17955 on a five-hour sortie, after which they recovered into Beale rather than Lockheed's Palmdale facility, where the jet had been

based. On 9 July, Rosenberg and McKim completed a seven-hour flight to Mildenhall, via the Barents/Baltic Seas collection area, in 64-17955.

Local British aeroplane spotters peering through binoculars and telescopes from various off-base vantage points excitedly recorded the 'Habu's' arrival. Some noted its slightly bumpy ASARS-1 nose, as well as an 'already familiar' tail number, which many people jotted down in their log books. On that occasion, however, all of them had logged a false serial, as a cover number was being used to conceal the fact that the test jet had been deployed overseas. As 64-17955 was already known by aviation enthusiasts as 'the Palmdale test ship', it had

been decided by the maintenance personnel at Beale to temporarily re-christen it 64-17962 for this deployment. The latter jet had previously visited Mildenhall on a number of occasions, and it would not therefore draw unwelcome attention, and speculation, to the unique test deployment of the ASARS-1 system.

On 18 July, Thomas and Morgan took the aircraft on a 2.6-hour ASARS-1 operational test sortie to monitor military installations in East Germany. Three days later, Rosenberg and McKim completed a four-hour mission. On the 22nd, Thomas and Morgan flew Det 4's second SR-71, 64-17980, to nearby Greenham Common for the 1983 Air Tattoo. Among the tens of thousands of people who came to see the aircraft were some of the 'Greenham Women', who had long been demonstrating against numerous political issues, and who had been camping outside the base to gain public recognition for their cause. The day before the SR-71 was due to return to Mildenhall, some of the demonstrators managed to daub white paint on it. They were quickly arrested for causing a disturbance, and for possible damage to the aircraft's titanium – laboratory analysis subsequently proved that it was unharmed.

Several days later, Maj Jim Jiggens and RSO Capt Joe McCue performed an unforgettable departure from the base. After a morning take-off on 26 July for the short flight back to Mildenhall, Jiggens (an ex-Thunderbirds airshow demonstration pilot, who had obtained prior

This radome, housing the C3 Com datalink antenna, was fitted to 64-17955 in 1983 along with the ASARS-1 equipment (*USAF*)

When Det 4 lost its TR-1s, the change was reflected in its redesigned operations location board (Paul F Crickmore)

Palmdale 'test-bird' 64-17955 is seen here in its normal markings, resplendent with the Lockheed Skunk – a scheme guaranteed to have provoked unwanted interest in the jet had it been so adorned when it arrived at Mildenhall (*Lockheed*)

64-17980 joined Det 4 from Beale on 7 March 1983, and it is seen here coming over the fence at RAF Greenham Common on 22 July, where it participated in that year's Air Tattoo (*Paul F Crickmore*)

Maj B C Thomas carries out post-flight checks of 64-17955 (*USAF*)

Surrounded by daisies, 64-17980 returned to Beale on 6 September 1983 (*Bob Archer*)

permission from the base commander to do a farewell flyby), flew a wide circular pattern at 250 knots towards the Greenham Peace Camp. As 64-17980 reached a strategic point, Jiggens pushed both throttles to full 'burner, whereupon the jet thundered over the encampment at very low altitude. Applying sharp back-pressure to the control column and lofting the 'Habu' into a spectacular climb, he allowed his aircraft to trumpet the 'sound of freedom' as only an SR-71 could.

The final ASARS-1 demonstration flight was conducted on 30 July, when Thomas and Morgan flew 64-17955 on a 7.3-hour flight back to Beale, via the Baltic/Barents Seas. The system had performed flawlessly throughout the deployment, proving that ASARS-1 represented a quantum leap in radar resolution and capability for reconnaissance purposes. Capts Gary Luloff and RSO Bob Coats ferried the aircraft back to Palmdale on 2 August, where further tests were conducted, prior to an initial order being placed with Goodyear for two production radar sets for the operational fleet.

PERMANENT DET

Although the 1983 deployment to Mildenhall was still called a 'temporary operation', two SR-71s remained on strength with Det 4 throughout the year (apart from a period lasting just 33 days in early 1983, and three days in the autumn).

As early as 1980, SAC had begun planning changes in the SR-71's European operations to cut the cost of deployments and to increase the frequency of surveillance flights. Such changes required actions of 'air diplomacy' on the part of HQ 3rd Air Force and USAF and SAC staff

specialists. Following orders from the JCS, HQ USAF and HQ SAC, Col Don Walbrecht of the 3rd Air Force, accompanied by Lt Col John Fuller and Lt Col Dwight Kealoa of HQ USAF/XOXX (Protectorate of Plans and Policy), and Lt Col Kenneth Hagemann of HQ SAC/XP (Deputy Chief of Staff Plans), proposed to Assistant Secretary Martin Scicluna and Gp Capt Frank Appleyard, Deputy Director of Operations in the RAF's Directorate of Organisation (DGO/RAF), that SR-71 operations at Mildenhall should be 'bedded down' on a permanent basis.

Scicluna (Head of the MoD's 5-9 (AIR)) led the British contingent who reviewed the proposal. Although he thought that the SR-71's high visibility image might cause 'political difficulties' at some senior levels, he took the issue forward to Secretary of State for Defence, Sir Francis Pym, who agreed to consider it. After specialised briefings to a handful of MoD 'insiders', including certain intelligence officers who had 'special access' to US reconnaissance information, their recommendations were taken to Pym, who agreed to the initiative. Another meeting held three days later worked out the politics of the proposal.

The following week, each member of the US team briefed his respective CINC or Deputy Chief of Staff in Ramstein, Omaha or Washington, DC that the programme was 'on track' in Whitehall. Soon after, Prime Minister Margaret Thatcher's approval was noted as a simple 'change of mode of operations' from temporary deployments to a permanent presence at RAF Mildenhall. U-2/TR-1 operations were also to be moved from Mildenhall to nearby RAF Alconbury as both bases were 'beefed-up' for their expanded intelligence roles.

On 5 April 1984, Prime Minister Thatcher announced that a permanent detachment of SR-71s had been established at the Suffolk base following the blanket clearance given by her government to the USAF to operate two 'Habus' from the UK. Nevertheless, certain sorties performed by Det 4 would still require prior high-level approval from the MoD. Moreover, those especially sensitive operations would require 'clearance' from the PM herself.

Anglo-American cooperation also extended to the performing of the actual SR-71 missions themselves. For example, 'Habu' sorties venturing into the Barents/Baltic Seas were occasionally timed to coincide with missions being flown in the same area by the RAF's trio of Nimrod R 1 ELINT aircraft, operated at that time by No 51 Sqn from RAF Wyton, in Huntingdonshire. Such cooperation also extended to the German *Marineflieger*, which used Breguet Atlantics to carry out a similar ELINT role to the Nimrod R 1s.

During such sorties, the SR-71 acted as the *provocateur*, with the on-station timings of both aircraft being controlled to within seconds so as to ensure that the slower ELINT platform was in the optimum position to take full advantage of signals traffic that was not usually forthcoming from the Soviet side.

64-17971 departs Mildenhall's runway 29 on 2 February 1983 at 230 knots and climbs away at an initial angle of attack of ten degrees. The gear-limit speed on take-off/ landing was 300 knots, which meant that prompt undercarriage retraction was necessary if damage to the doors was to be avoided. Shock diamonds in the exhaust plume are clearly visible in the clear, crisp winter air (*Bob Archer*)

'HABU' AND THE OPPOSITION

Immediately after World War 2, it was clear that two major geo-political systems would dominate the world. Inherent in both was their mutually abiding mistrust of the other, which in turn sowed the seeds for an arms race that would continue until one system achieved dominance over the other. Soviet intelligence concerning the development of USAF high-speed, high altitude bombers and reconnaissance platforms like the Convair B-58 Hustler, North American B-70 Valkyrie and Lockheed SR-71 inevitably provoked a self-perpetuating cause and effect response with the opposing power bloc.

As early as 1960, the Mikoyan-Gurevich Opytno-Konstruktorskoye Byuro (OKB design bureau) was tasked with developing a multi-role supersonic interceptor that was capable of defeating these new and emerging threats then under development in the US. The end result was the first 'big MiG' – the outstanding MiG-25 'Foxbat'.

The Soviets also embarked upon the development of the improved S-200 medium- to high-altitude SAM system. Designated the SA-5 'Gammon' by NATO, it represented a considerable advance over the SA-2 'Guideline'. The single-stage missile consisted of four jettisonable, wraparound solid propellant boosters, giving it a range of up to 300 km, a maximum altitude of between 20,000 and 40,000 metres, depending upon the variant, and a top speed of 2500 metres per second. Equipped with a 215-kg high explosive warhead, the SA-5 entered service in 1967.

Just two years later, it was estimated that 75 SA-5 battalions had been deployed around the nation's military bases, industrial complexes and population centres. Each missile battalion was equipped with between two and five trainable, semi-fixed single rail launchers and one 320-km range P-35M 'Barlock-B' E/F-band target search and acquisition radar that also boasted an integral D-band IFF (Identification Friend or Foe) system. Target tracking and missile guidance were handled by a 5N62 'Square Pair' H-band radar that had a range of 270 km. Once launched, the missiles were command guided until switched to semi-active mode for terminal homing to the target.

Five years after the SA-5 had entered service, the establishment of the first MiG-25P unit was officially announced by the Soviet air force (VVS) in a directive dated 13 April 1972. Initially, Protective Air Defence (PVO) units were stationed near Moscow, Kiev, Perm, Baku, Rostov and in the northern and far eastern regions of the USSR. By the mid-1970s, 600+ MiG-25Ps constituted the backbone of the VVS's interceptor inventory. Soon after converting to type, PVO units stationed near Soviet border areas were carrying out intercepts of SR-71s involved in peripheral reconnaissance missions of the USSR.

The mighty MiG-25PD/PDS 'Foxbat-E' posed a serious threat to Det 4's operations over the Barents/Baltic Seas. SR-71s conducting reconnaissance missions in this area were primarily opposed by interceptors from the 787th IAP. The unit was equipped with the MiG-25PD from July 1982 through to August 1989 (*VVS*)

On 6 September 1976, 'Foxbat' pilot Lt Victor Belenko from a PVO unit at Chuguyevka air base, north of Vladivostok, defected to the West via Japan in 'his' MiG-25P. This totally unexpected turn of events provided the US intelligence community with a 'windfall', and the aircraft was virtually dismantled by USAF intelligence analysts. Although the interceptor was later returned to its country of origin, it was obvious to Soviet officials that the MiG-25P's capabilities had now been severely compromised. Indeed, unless the design was drastically upgraded, the type's combat efficiency would be enormously degraded.

In a joint effort that involved the Ministry of Aircraft Industry and military experts, the Mikoyan OKB embarked upon a comprehensive upgrade programme. The jet's earlier monopulse low-pulse repetition frequency (PRF) 'Smerch-A2' (Izdelye 720M) radar was replaced by the much-improved 'Sapfeer-25'. This new system was larger than its predecessor, which in turn meant that a modest fuselage stretch forward of the cockpit was required in order to facilitate its accommodation. The radar's improved capabilities allowed the aircraft to detect targets with a Radar Cross Section of 16 m^2 at a range of more than 100 km (62.5 miles).

An infra-red search and track (IRST) system was also developed which, when coupled with the radar, made the weapons system less susceptible to the effects of enemy ECM. It also provided the platform with the capability to perform 'sneak attacks' against aerial targets without the pilot having to first switch on the radar.

The upgrade also included the installation of the BAN-75 target indication and guidance system, which acted in concert with the ground-based Luch-1 ('Ray') guidance system to align the optical axis of the aircraft's radar with the target. This also ensured that the MiG-25's radar was less sensitive to jamming. In addition, a new IFF set and ground-based command system were also provided – the latter, which replaced the Vozdookh-1M, incorporated a jam-proof aircraft receiver.

Four R-60 (AA-8 'Aphid') air-to-air missiles (AAMs) could be carried, which due to more effective homing heads had almost double the range of earlier weapons. R-40TD (AA-7 'Acrid') IR-homing and R-40R active-radar homing AAMs remained in the MiG-25's arsenal too. Finally, and perhaps not surprisingly, the upgraded platform would be powered by the improved version of the Tumanskii R-15 engine, designated the R-15BD-300.

Work progressed rapidly on the fighter, which was designated the MiG-25PD or Izdelye 84D (D standing for *Dorabotannyy* in Cyrillic, which meant modified or upgraded in English). The new version replaced the MiG-25P on the production line in 1978, and examples were delivered to the VVS through to late 1982. Some 370 MiG-25Ps were also subjected to a mid-life update programme between 1979 and 1984, leading to them being redesignated MiG-25PDSs (*Perekhvatchik, Doralotannyy v Stroyou*, or field-modified interceptor).

FRONTLINE FIGHTER OPERATIONS

An insight into MiG-25PD operations as conducted by the 787th IAP (*Istrebitelniy Aviatsionniy Polk*, or Fighter Aviation Regiment) against Det 4 SR-71s flying over the Baltic Sea is reproduced here courtesy of Lutz Freund, editor of *Sowjetische Fliegerkrafte Deutschland 1945-1994*;

'Between 14 July 1982 and 10 August 1989, the 787th IAP flew the MiG-25PD. This was more or less the same period of time that the SR-71 operated out of Mildenhall. With the retirement of the SR-71 from the UK, the 787th IAP replaced its MiG-25PDs with MiG-23s and MiG-29s. The regiment operated its MiGs from Finow-Eberswalde air base in the German Democratic Republic (GDR). This airfield had originally been built for the Luftwaffe in 1936, and it was used by Soviet forces from 1945. With the introduction of the MiG-25PU two-seat trainer, Finow-Eberswalde's runway (10/28) was enlarged to 2510 m.

'In 1980, Warsaw Pact PVO units introduced a new alarm call – "Jastreb" (hawk). It meant that an SR-71 was approaching! Later on, it became the standard alarm signal for all high and very fast flying targets. Under normal circumstances the alarm call came several minutes before a SR-71, with its typical flight parameters at an altitude of 20 to 25 kilometres and flying at some 800-900 metres a second, entered the range of Soviet and GDR radar air surveillance and radar guidance troops. In parallel, this alarm prompted action at Finow-Eberswalde which usually resulted in the in the scrambling of MiG-25PDs from the 787th IAP.

'The interceptors took off and approached the intruder by flying a wide curve on a parallel course, separated by a few kilometres. When performing this manoeuvre, the MiG-25 pilots had to use all the airspace available to them over either the northern or southern GDR. On all military maps the MiG-25's flight path was shown as a big circle.

'When the weather was favourable, SR-71s flew reconnaissance missions once or twice a week along the Warsaw Pact border. During military

64-17975 only deployed to Det 4 once, between mid-July and 16 October 1984. Having just cleared the 'piano keys', the aircraft is just seconds from touch down on Mildenhall's runway 11. This aircraft flew a number of Barents/Baltic Seas missions during its time in the UK (*Paul F Crickmore*)

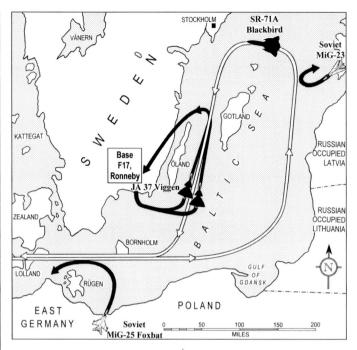

**This map reveals the standard
course followed by SR-71 crews
when overflying the Baltic Sea,
as well as the typical 'engagement'
zones employed by VVS MiG-25PDs
and MiG-31s and Swedish Air Force
JA 37 Viggens when tasked with
intercepting the high-flying 'Habu'**
(*Osprey*)

manoeuvres, flight frequency could
increase to two missions per 24 hours.
For all of these SR-71 flights,
there were two standard routes.
The aircraft usually approached
GDR airspace from Denmark. Over
the West German city of Kiel, the
flight path continued either to *Aufklärungsstrecke* 2 (reconnaissance route
2), which was along the Baltic sea coast
to Leningrad (now St Peterburg)
and back, or to *Aufklärungsstrecke* 5
(reconnaissance route), along the
GDR's western border. Such missions
usually took 60 minutes to complete.
The distance to the border varied due
to theaircraft's high velocity – it was
unable to follow the exact borderline.
Sometimes, an SR-71 closed up to
within a few kilometres of the GDR's
border in the area of Boizenburg, or
just slipped over it!

'Had there ever been an order to shoot down the intruder, the
MiG-25 crews would have been ready. Fortunately, such an order was
never given. After a short time flying next to each other, the MiG-25PDs
headed home to Finow-Eberswalde via Polish airspace.

'Beside the airborne defenders, missile defence forces would have also
been placed in alarm status. Technically, it would have been possible to
successfully destroy the intruder, although the SA-5 battery would have
needed the SR-71 to fly laterally to the missile's launch ramp for a short
while so as to improve the weapon's chances of attaining a successful
lock-on at the extreme altitude at which the jet made its reconnaissance
runs. The missile air defence force was kept at full alert whilst the SR-71
was being tracked by Soviet radio-listening systems.'

In 1972, the Mikoyan OKB began working on a new interceptor
destined to replace the MiG-25. Designed around two powerful
Aviadvigatel D-30F6 afterburning turbofans, the aircraft would have both
a lower top speed and ceiling than the MiG-25PD. However, this fourth
generation fighter was equipped with a weapons control system based on
the SBI-16 Zaslon ('Flash Dance') phased-array radar, enabling its two
crewmembers to intercept targets in either the front or rear hemisphere, day
or night, in any weather conditions, whilst operating in a passive or an active
jamming environment at high supersonic speeds. Cleared for construction
in late 1979, the MiG-31's final Act of Acceptance was signed in December
1981 and the first examples were delivered to PVO units in 1982.
Codenamed the 'Foxhound' by NATO, some 500 examples had been
delivered to the VVS by the time production ended in 1989.

Like the MiG-25PD before it, the new MiG also had a full IRST
capability. Located in a retractable pod beneath the forward fuselage, the
Type 8TP IRST enabled the aircraft to execute attacks without recourse to
its radar. Typical armament consisted of four R-33 long-range air-to-air

missiles carried semi-recessed in the fuselage on AKU-410 ejector racks, or four R-60M missiles if the target was to be engaged using the IRST. Each R-33 weighed 1058 lbs, including its 103-lb HE/fragmentation warhead, and had a range of 75 miles.

The new Zaslon radar touted a detection range of 180 km (111 miles) and a target tracking range of 120 km (75 miles). The aircraft's avionics suite also included the BAN-75 command link, the SAU-155M automatic flight control system, the APD-518 digital secure data link system (which enabled a flight of four MiG-31s to swap data generated by their radars provided that they were within 200 km (124 miles) of one another), the RK-RLDN secure data link and the SPO-15SL Radar Homing And Warning System. Finally, the jet's superior navigation suite allowed the crew to safely patrol the barren Arctic theatre of operations.

By late 1980 the 'Foxhound's' flight test programme had been successfully completed, and within two years the first MiG-31 production aircraft had been delivered to PVO units. The latter had achieved initial operating capability by mid-1982. The major units to be equipped with the type were the 153rd IAP, stationed at Morshansk, the 786th IAP at Pravdinsk, the 180th IAP at Gromovo, the 174th GvIAP at Monchegorsk, the 72nd IAP at Amderma and the 518th IAP at Talagi.

Russian writer Valery Romanenko has undertaken detailed research for this book, piecing together a unique insight into MiG-31 operations against Det 4 SR-71s. The fruits of that effort are detailed below;

'Military 1st Class Pilot Guards Maj Mikhail Myagkiy (ret.), was one of the PVO pilots who executed intercepts of the SR-71 near the far northern borders of the USSR. Between 1984 and 1987, he was a MiG-31 "Foxhound" commander with the 174th GvIAP (*Gvardeiskaya Istrebitelniy Aviatsionniy Polk*, or Guards Fighter Aviation Regiment). During this period Myagkiy conducted 14 successful SR-71 intercepts.

'A graduate of the Armavir VVAKUL PVO (Higher Military Aviation Red Banner Academy of Pilots of the PVO) in 1977, Myagkiy commenced his frontline service flying the Sukhoi Su-15 "Flagon". He then qualified as a 1st Class Pilot on the MiG-23ML "Flogger-G", having by then accumulated approximately 600 hours of total flying time and been promoted to the rank of captain.

'In 1983, only two regiments flew the MiG-31. The 786th IAP at Pravdinsk (near Gorkiy) had been the first regiment to receive the "Foxhound", followed by the 174th GvIAP at Monchegorsk (near Murmansk). Prior to being issued with the MiG-31, the 174th GvIAP had flown the Yakovlev Yak-28P 'Firebar'. During the transition to the MiG-31, many pilots left the unit – they did not want to fly the new aircraft. With most of the regiment's remaining trainees being weapon systems operators (WSOs), the PVO had to select pilots from other units in order to bring the 174th GvIAP back up to strength once again. At that time only 1st Class pilots were being selected to fly the MiG-31, so just a small number of aviators were qualified to join the regiment.

'The PVO's 14th Air Army was required to supply one pilot to the 10th Air Army, to which the 174th GvIAP was assigned. This proved to be Capt Myagkiy. As an acting flight commander, a transfer to the 174th GvIAP meant a reduction in rank for him since the 14th Air Army commander refused to release Myagkiy from his permanent duty position. Indeed, he only allowed his pilots to transfer to temporary positions within other Air Armies. Myagkiy joined the 174th GvIAP in October 1983. The regiment had been equipped with the MiG-31 for 18 months by then, and its crews had frequently flown missions against the SR-71.

'After a month at Monchegorsk, Myagkiy was sent to the TsBP IA-PVO (*Tsentry Boyevoy Podgotovki* – centre for combat readiness, PVO fighter aviation) in Savasleyka for MiG-31 transition training. The WSOs, two of whom Myagkiy would later fly with, also underwent transition training at Savasleyka. Over the course of two months, the pilots were taught to fly the MiG-25PU "Foxbat-C" and MiG-31 (students took a separate examination on each aircraft). Initially, they completed four flights in dual-control MiG-25PU two-seater trainers, and their fifth, sixth and seventh sorties in the MiG-31 (with an instructor). On the eighth flight the pilots went solo (with a WSO in the back seat, rather than an instructor). Having successfully gone solo on the "Foxhound", pilots completed all their remaining training flights in the MiG-31.

'The flight-training programme was very short. On 21 May 1984, Capt Myagkiy received his authorisation for independent flights in the MiG-31, and on 21 June he was deemed to be combat ready. This meant that he could now perform a combat air patrol in daytime and in bad weather. By the end of July Myagkiy was carrying out frontline patrols.

'His first mission against the SR-71 came on 21 August 1984. According to Myagkiy, the procedures followed by the regiment in an attempt to perform a successful intercept were totally inadequate when it came to negating the threat posed by the SR-71's spy flights. The speed and altitude of the US aircraft simply hypnotised everyone in the VVS. Therefore, each attempted SR-71 interception was considered a top priority, not only for fighter aviation but also for the PVO's entire 10th Air Army.

'The ground vectoring station on the Rybachiy Peninsula often made the first "sighting". Intercepting jets then took off from bases in the north that were not weather affected. An error at any level – by aircrew, groundcrew, those in the command post or by a ground vectoring station controller – brought with it the threat of a military tribunal (court martial).

Making its frontline debut with the PVO in 1982, the MiG-31 'Foxhound' represented an extremely capable adversary for the SR-71 – especially when equipped with R-33 air-to-air missiles as seen here under the belly of 'Blue 31' (*Yefim Gordon*)

Between 21 August 1984 and 8 January 1987, 174th GvIAP pilot Maj Mikhail Myagkiy (right) conducted 14 practice intercepts on SR-71s whilst at the controls of a MiG-31 'Foxhound'. Most of these took place over the Barents Sea, Myagkiy having been scrambled from the 174th GvIAP's base at Monchegorsk, near Murmansk (*Mikhail Myagkiy*)

64-17973 taxies back to its 'barn' at Mildenhall in May 1987, the jet's brake 'chute doors still in the open position. The 'chute was usually ejected by the pilot whilst decelerating during the roll-out through 55 knots to ensure that its heavy attachment point was pulled clear of the aft fuselage without damaging the SR-71 (*Paul F Crickmore*)

'Each fighter regiment executed intercepts in their own sector. For the 174th GvIAP, this was the sector of the Soviet border from Kharlovka to Cape Svyatoy Nos. For the unit's MiG-31 crews, 16 minutes usually elapsed from the moment the alert was sounded to the take-off command being given.

'Of this time, two minutes were used by the pilot and WSO to don their VKK-3 (*vysotnyy kompensiruyushchiy kostyum*, or altitude-compensating suit) flightsuits, followed by two more minutes to run 60 m (66 yards) in the VKK and get strapped into the jet. The remainder of the time was then spent checking out the MiG-31's various systems, starting the engines and taxiing to the runway threshold. After 16 minutes the fighter would be parked at the end of the runway, with its engines running, fully prepared for take-off.

'When the SR-71 alert was first given, the technical personnel would run to the jet and remove its R-60 short-range missiles, as these could not be fired at speeds exceeding Mach 1.75 – the standard MiG-31 ordnance load consisted of four R-60s and four long-range R-33s.

'Prior to the aircraft taking off, its inertial navigation system (INS) had to be activated in minimum time. As soon as the green lights came on in the cockpits confirming that the INS was aligned (after approximately three minutes), the engines could be fired up.

'Sat in their cockpits, the minutes ticking away, the pilots and WSOs of the ready flight had to complete their pre-flight checks in a somewhat tense environment. The MiG-31s assigned to the 174th GvIAP were from the first production series, and they were prone to suffering from systems failure – particularly during the turning off of ground power once the "Foxhound's" engines had fired up. If the ground power plug was pulled out too abruptly, the INS system malfunctioned. The crew that managed to reach full mission readiness first was the one that launched.

'Having received permission to taxi, the aircraft took up its position at the end of the runway. Here, crews sometimes had to "cool their jets" for several minutes if they had reached the runway ahead of the allocated departure time. The SR-71 intercept profile adopted by the PVO had been computed down to the very last second, which in turn meant that the MiG-31s had to launch exactly 16 minutes after the initial alert was sounded. By then the ground vectoring station had determined precisely what route (out route or return route) the SR-71 was following.

'Five minutes after take-off, the MiG-31 was already at an altitude of 16,000 m (52,493 ft). The afterburners would still be lit and the crew experiencing significant G-forces. Additionally, the MiG-31 had a disconcerting idiosyncrasy. At high supersonic speeds (above Mach 2.35), the control column moved all the way forward, pushing up against the instrument panel. The pilot had to fully extend his arm in order to remain in control of the jet. Fatigue would soon set in if the pilot was forced to keep his arm outstretched for more than a few minutes at a time. Despite this peculiar problem, the MiG-31 was far more benign in its flight characteristics at supersonic speeds than the MiG-25. The great weight of the MiG-31's onboard equipment and systems all had an adverse effect on its top end performance in comparison with the "Foxbat", but its avionics were vastly superior to those fitted in the MiG-25.

'During an SR-71 intercept, many commonly accepted practices were broken. For example, take-off was executed in a northerly direction, while normal procedure called for a take-off to the south. A number of limitations were also removed, including the altitude for transition to supersonic flight. Established as 11,000 m (36,089 ft) during a routine flight, when a MiG-31 crew was intercepting an SR-71, Soviet aircraft were permitted to pass through the sound barrier at just 8000 m (26,247 ft). Finally, ground vectoring was usually conducted at an altitude of 16,000 m (52,493 ft), but when going after an SR-71, the MiG-31 could reach altitudes of 18,500-19,500 m (60,696-63,976 ft). In an attempt to establish the best missile launch trajectory, the MiG crews gained as much altitude as they could – often up to a height of 20,000 m (65,617 ft).

'Soviet radio intercept stations usually started receiving information about an inbound SR-71 when it was three hours out. As the jet departed Mildenhall, conversations between its crew and those manning supporting KC-135Qs were "captured" during inflight refuelling. Highly trained radio intercept operators knew that if the tankers showed up, the PVO needed to be told that an SR-71 was heading for the Barents/Baltic Seas.

'The standard SR-71 route was normally loop shaped. If the jet appeared from the direction of Norway, it tracked toward the White Sea, headed further north toward Novaya Zemlya and then turned around on a reverse course to the west over the Arctic Ocean. This track was called a "straight loop". However, if it initially approached from the direction of the Arctic Ocean toward Novaya Zemlya, then headed south toward the White Sea and west along the coast of the USSR toward Norway, its track was called the "return loop". The tactics employed by the MiG-31 crew were geared toward the type of loop the spyplane was flying.

'The SR-71 was intercepted using only a thermal channel (infra-red, IR), as the massive IR emissions of its engines meant that the jet could be detected at a distance of 100-120 km (62-75 miles). The MiG-31's thermal detection system was called OMB (optical multi-functional apparatus), and was mounted in the lower nose of the aircraft. The device was lowered and turned on by the WSO, whilst the MiG's radar remained inactive throughout the interception. When on a combat alert the radar was set on a combat frequency. However, the VVS was keen not to expose this frequency to a "probable enemy" during a routine SR-71 intercept, so the radar was not turned on – all SR-71 flights were supported by RC-135 ELINT/SIGINT platforms attempting to collect frequencies such as this. A passive system such as the OMB fitted to the MiG-31 was more than adequate to ensure that the SR-71 was intercepted.

'After capture of the target by the OMB, a target indicator showing the range to the SR-71 appeared on the SEI (*sistema edinoy indikatsii*, or unified display system) in the pilot's head-up display (HUD). A female voice (known as "Rita" to the crews) indicator announced "Attack!" The range to the target was calculated by the aircraft's BTsVM (or onboard digital computer), using a triangulation method that employed other on-board sensors. This system was unique to the MiG-31, for the pilot did not receive range-to-target data in the MiG-25 – he had to rely on data passed from ground vectoring stations instead. Also, the ZDR (missile engagement envelope) was projected onto the HUD.

'After being given the "Attack!" signal, the crew began missile preparation. Targeting instructions were handed off to the GSN (*golovka samonavedeniya*, or the target-seeking device of the missile – i.e. its seeker head). Four green triangles appeared on the image of the MiG in the cockpit display after the missiles had been prepared for launch.

'The BRLS (*bortovaya radiolokatsionnaya stantsiya*, or on-board radar) was turned on only in the event that the vectoring station issued an order to destroy the target. In this case, the WSO would activate the radar. Information regarding the target would then be instantly transferred from the OMB to the radar. After this the pilot had only to push the firing button and the missiles would be launched.

'If the SR-71 had violated Soviet airspace, a live missile launch would have been carried out – there was practically no chance that the aircraft could avoid an R-33. But in the early 1980s the SR-71 did not violate the border, although they sometimes "tickled" it (came right up to it). Indeed, local counter-intelligence officers dreamt of finding pieces of an SR-71, if not on land then in the territorial waters of the USSR.'

Of all the intercept missions flown by Mikhail Myagkiy in the MiG-31, his eighth one stands out the most, as he managed to gain visual contact with an SR-71 – and not just in the form of a dot on his windscreen. As a keepsake, he preserved the printout of the recording from the 'black box' through which all the intercept data was processed. Here is how Myagkiy described the flight;

'I went on combat alert on 31 January 1986 as normal. I drew my personal weapon in the morning and then headed for the on-duty crew hut.

'They alerted us about an inbound SR-71 at 1100 hrs. They sounded the alarm with a shrill bell and then confirmed it with a loudspeaker. To this day I have been averse even to ordinary school bells, because a bell was the first signal for a burst of adrenaline. The appearance of an SR-71 was always accompanied by nervousness. Everyone began to talk in frenzied voices, to scurry about and react to the situation with excessive emotion.

Although deployed to Mildenhall just once, 64-17960 served with Det 4 for no less than 15 months, from 29 October 1985 through to 29 January 1987. It was almost certainly intercepted by 174th GvIAP pilot Maj Mikhail Myagkiy over the Barents Sea during this time (*Paul F Crickmore*)

All buttoned-down and with its systems fully operable, 64-17964 prepares to leave the Det 4 'barn' on a Barents/Baltic Seas sortie on 17 December 1987 (*Paul F Crickmore*)

'I ran to put on my VKK and GSh-6 (*germoshlem*, or flight helmet), and over that a fur-lined flight jacket with IPS (*individualnaya podvesnaya systema*, or parachute harness), then ran 60 m to the aircraft. I was not flying with my own WSO, but with Aleksey Parshin, our flight WSO. I sat down in the cockpit, and as I was being strapped in – it was both simple and convenient to be strapped in wearing a jacket and IPS, which is why we flew in them – the readiness lamps for the INS were lit. I pressed the engine start button, reported to the command post and immediately received the order to taxi to the runway. We sat on the runway for five minutes, my WSO loudly "reading the prayer" (pre-take-off checklist).

'After receiving the take-off order from the command post, we lit the afterburners and took off. Our take-off speed was approximately 360 kmh (224 mph). Remaining in afterburners, we went for altitude with a 60-degree right bank, followed by a turn onto a course of 100°. We attained 8000 m (26,247 ft) and reached the horizontal area (for acceleration), at which point we passed through the sound barrier. Vectoring station "Gremikha" had by then assumed responsibility for guiding us to the SR-71. Our indicated speed at this time was 1190 kmh (739 mph). We went for altitude again, up to 16,000 m (52,493 ft).

'Once at 16,000 m we were flying at Mach 2.3, and I made a left turn onto a combat course of 360°. The WSO lowered and turned on the OMB, and within five seconds he had captured the target. A feminine voice in the earphones announced, "Attack!", and a symbol was illuminated on the SEI. The SR-71 was proceeding on the "return loop", from east to west, so we began the intercept immediately.

'As usual, we executed an "aiming run" from 16,000 m, gaining altitude to 18,900 m (62,008 ft). After closing to within 60 km (37 miles) of the target, I spotted the contrail of the SR-71 on an intersecting course. I reported the heading to my WSO over the SPU (*samoletnoye peregovornoye ustroystvo*, or intercom), then told him "I have visual!" A contrail at 22,000-23,000 m (69,000-72,000 ft) is very rare, but on this day the weather was excellent and the air was transparent, making the contrail clearly visible. I passed under the spyplane, which was 3000-4000 m (8843-13,123 ft) above us, and I even managed to make out its black silhouette. The SR-71 was flying over the ocean ever so carefully on a track 60 km (37 miles) out from, and parallel to, the coast. I reported "We're breaking off" to the command post and came off afterburners. We had been airborne for just 15 minutes and 40 seconds.

'The SR-71 was flying its normal route over neutral waters, and it made no sense to follow it. Therefore, the vectoring station gave us the command to turn onto a course for our airfield. We dropped down to 15,000 m (49,213 ft), transitioned to horizontal flight and engaged a stopwatch. This was the so-called "area for canopy cooling". During flight at speeds in excess of Mach 2, the skin, including the canopy, heated up to 800°C (1472°F). Therefore, it was necessary to cool it. Failure to do so might result in cracking or catastrophic failure during subsequent altitude reduction. Our speed remained in the order of Mach 1.6.

'After 30 seconds we once again began to lose altitude. We went subsonic at 12,000 m (39,370 ft). Dropping down to 8000 m (26,247 ft), we tracked toward our airfield. After the last vector was issued, the command centre handed us off to our regimental command post, which directed us to a checkpoint at an altitude of 4100 m (13,451 ft). At 32 km (20 miles) out from the airfield, I lowered the gear and began to descend. We conducted a straight-in landing at a speed of 310 kmh (193 mph). The entire flight had lasted 50 minutes.

'During the 15 to 20 minutes that I was on a combat course, the second alert crew was sitting on the ground with engines running. Later, they shut down their engines, but the pilot and WSO sat in their aircraft at a state of readiness until we had landed.

'This was the only occasion in my 14 intercepts that I saw the SR-71 with my own eyes. It was obvious that a combination of circumstances facilitated this event – good weather, which was rare in the north, clear air and unusual atmospheric conditions, which meant that the jet's contrail was clearly visible at an altitude of 23,000 m (75,459 ft).'

Mikhail Myagkiy retired from the VVS in 1992 with the rank of Guards Major at the age of 36.

MONITORING INTERCEPTS

Retired Swedish air force fighter controller Rolf Jonsson routinely monitored SR-71 intercepts conducted by both friendly NATO aircraft and not so friendly Soviet MiG-25s and MiG-31s whilst the 'Habu' was operating over the Baltic Sea;

'We would detect possible SR-71 "Baltic Express" flights about an hour before the aircraft physically entered the area. The "Habu" always headed into the Baltic Sea over a reporting point named "Codan", located about 50 miles (80 km) south of Copenhagen, and on a heading of about 90°. This usually triggered a scramble by a pair of JA 37 Viggens that were kept on alert at F10 Angelholm, F17 Ronneby and F13 Norrköping – sometimes, jets operating from temporary bases such as Visby were also used. The perfect base from which to launch an SR-71 interception was F17 Ronneby because it was best positioned for the acceleration and climb phase due to it being just 31 miles (50 km) southeast of Gotland.

'The SR-71's Baltic flightpath remained the same throughout the time it operated in Europe, consisting of a single anticlockwise loop that took about 30 minutes to complete. It remained in international airspace, initially flying along the Polish coastline. As it approached the Bay of Gdanska, well inside the Kalingrad enclave, the jet turned left onto a heading of 015°. With the "Habu" now flying at 80,000 ft (24,384 m), only the Su-15 "Flagons" based at Vainode, in Latvia, had a chance of making an intercept, and it's doubtful that any of them were actually successful. Certainly the MiG-21 "Fishbeds" and MiG-23 "Floggers" based at Pamu, Haapsalu and Tapa, in Estonia, had no chance – their trails on our radar screens in Sweden were so harmless it was painful!

'The "Habu" then proceeded to a point about 37 miles (60 km) west of the Estonian island of Saaremaa, where it began a long, programmed left turn, taking it onto a southerly heading of about 190 °, before rolling out east of Stockholm. It then passed between the islands of Gotland and Oland, and this always impressed us because the corridor of international airspace between the two islands is only two miles wide. The "Habu" only violated our airspace once (this was the only time that it became necessary for the Swedish foreign office to protest about an airspace violation) when an SR-71 was forced to interrupt its high speed left turn, reduce speed and descend from its operational ceiling due to an in-flight emergency. On that occasion, the SR-71 was forced to fly directly over Gotland, at which point JA 37 Viggen pilots took hand-held photos of the "Habu". From them it

JA 37 pilots managed to fly hazardous interception profiles which brought them within range of cruising SR-71s over the Baltic Sea. Although the Viggen, if carefully managed, had the ability to get within striking range of the 'Habu', the performance of its SkyFlash missiles in such an engagement is open to debate. This aircraft, from F13, is armed with SkyFlash (inboard) and Sidewinder air-to-air missiles (*Artech/Aerospace*)

Having completed their EGT checks, and with the wheel chocks still in place under the mains, the crew of 64-17964 hold on runway 29 in readiness for another pre-dawn departure (*Paul F Crickmore*)

was clear to see that the aircraft was flying on just one engine.

'It was in this area that our JA 37 pilots carried out their practice intercepts. Once 46 miles (74 km) southeast of land, the "Baltic Express" turned onto a heading of 265° and exited the area over the same point that it had entered.

'Almost every time the SR-71 was about to leave the Baltic, a lone MiG-25PD "Foxbat-E" belonging to the VVS's 787th IAP would be scrambled. The 787th maintained three squadrons (around 40 aircraft) at Finow-Eberswalde, all of which may have flown the MiG-25PD. It seems likely, however, that two of the units were equipped with MiG-23M "Flogger-Bs" and one with MiG-25PDs. A detachment of the latter aircraft was also maintained at Wittstock, and a second flight may have also been based at another airfield in southern GDR.

'When it arrived at its exit point, the "Baltic Express" was flying at about 72,000 ft (21,946 m). The lone MiG-25PD sent up to intercept the SR-71 would reach about 63,000 ft (19,202 m) in a left turn, before rolling out and completing its stern attack some 1.8 miles (2.9 km) behind its target. We were always impressed by this precision – the "Foxbat" was always 63,000 ft and 1.8 miles behind the SR-71.

'When the SR-71 detachment at Mildenhall was deactivated, the 787th IAP re-equipped with new MiG-29 "Fulcrum-Cs". Even after the reconnaissance aircraft's withdrawal from the UK, our intelligence sources indicated that at least three MiG-25PDs remained behind at Finow-Eberswalde just in case the "Baltic Express" returned!'

It is interesting to note when reading Rolf Jonsson's account involving a lone MiG-25PD out of Finow-Eberswalde that the simulated attack always terminated when the interceptor was at 63,000 ft and 1.8 miles behind its target. This would suggest that these were the parameters necessary for its weapons system to effect a successful intercept if the order to fire was ever given. This will, of course, forever remain supposition.

INTERCEPTION

It was rare for SR-71 crews to spot their pursuers during Barents/Baltic Seas operations, for a fully functioning 'Habu' would remain out of reach of any NATO or Soviet interceptor. However, a jet with technical issues (or the onset of freak weather conditions) could bring the SR-71 back to within reach of chasing fighters. This happened to Majs 'Stormy' Boudreaux and RSO Ted Ross, who departed Mildenhall in 64-17980 at 1010 hrs on 3 June 1986 on yet another Barents/Baltic Seas sortie.

Heading out across the North Sea toward their first refuelling west of Norway, the crew discovered once they were in the tanker track at 26,000 ft that the sun was directly ahead of them. To make matters worse, they were flanked on either side by clouds. As they closed for contact with the KC-135s, the cloud both diffused and angled the sunlight, causing the latter to reflect brightly off the bottom of the tankers.

As soon as the boomer made contact, Boudreaux found himself flying formation in almost blinding conditions, with the SR-71's cockpit instruments obscured in the dark shadow of the dashboard below the windscreen. He was forced to arrange his tiltable car-like sun-visor to shield against the high contrast conditions. That effort proved of little value, for while in the contact position 'on the boom', the tanker's reference points for formation flying were flashing in such extreme contrast that, according to Boudreaux, they appeared to be surrounded by 'sea, sky or whatever'. A strong sensation of vertigo overtook Boudreaux, leaving him with a false sense of diving and climbing (and with the even more powerful sensation of flying inverted while refuelling). An interphone call to his WSO, Maj Ross, assured Boudreaux that he was not upside-down. He was then able to continue filling 64-17980's tanks while fighting his sense of flying 'straight up or straight down'.

After clearing the tanker, and his senses, Boudreaux climbed through 60,000 ft, where he noted through his periscope that 64-17980 was still pulling contrails, which should have stopped above that altitude. Another check at 70,000 ft revealed that he was 'still conning', which he hoped would surely stop before they approached the target area. Upon entering the Barents Sea zone, the aircraft began a programmed left turn to the northeast and then reversed in a large sweeping right turn to roll out on a westerly heading, which would take the SR-71 on the 'collection run' and back across the entry point.

When established on the westerly heading north of Archangel, the crew noted that they were still 'conning', which was most abnormal at high altitudes. To add to their dismay, Boudreaux spotted three other contrails ahead of them and off to the left, but turning to converge in what might be an intercept. Another southerly glance revealed more 'cons' closing from the left, but at a lower altitude. These six Soviet fighters, each separated by approximately 15 miles, were executing what appeared to be a well-rehearsed turning intercept manoeuvre to pop up somewhere in the vicinity of the fast-moving 'Habu' and potentially fire off sophisticated air-to-air missiles. The Soviet fighter pilots had executed an in-place turn, which would have positioned them perfectly for a head-on attack had 64-17980's track penetrated Soviet airspace. As Ross monitored the fighters' electronic activities, Boudreaux increased speed and altitude.

Suddenly, a contrail shot by just beneath the nose of the SR-71, leaving both crewmembers waiting for a missile or another aircraft to appear which might have 'spoiled their whole day'. It was with great relief that Boudreaux realised that they were now paralleling their inbound contrail – they had laid it while turning northeast prior to heading west! For a few moments their hearts missed several beats as they contemplated the thought of having unwanted high-Mach company 15 miles above the cold Arctic seas.

Boudreaux eased off some power and settled the SR-71 back into a routine high-Mach cruise, the autopilot completing a long 'lazy turn' around the north shore of Norway before the pilot started his descent toward another refuelling. To complete the mission, the crew made an easy high altitude dash into the Baltic corridor and down through West Germany, before heading home to Mildenhall.

MIDDLE EAST AND SHUTDOWN

By the mid-1970s, the Middle East's complicated politics that had bonded Christian and Muslim factions together in relative peace in Lebanon since that country had declared its independence in November 1943 had broken down. Soon after, a long and tragic civil war erupted which was further complicated by the wider implications of the region's power politics. In an effort to restore peace, President Assad of Syria despatched more than 40,000 of his best troops to support the Palestine Liberation Organisation (PLO), and various other Muslim groups in the area, in a series of fruitless battles against Christian militias. In August 1982, the grim catalogue of human carnage had reached many thousands dead on both sides of the rising conflict.

Some 15 terrorist organisations sympathetic to the Palestinian cause operated from numerous bases in southern Lebanon, and periodically launched attacks against neighbouring Israel. These acts of terrorism became progressively more numerous and violent. After several retaliatory strikes, Israel responded on 6 June 1982 with a major land, sea and air invasion aimed at destroying the PLO leadership, and its armed forces. Twenty-three days later, Israeli troops had reached the outskirts of Beirut, and were in a position to fulfil their stated objective. Although the Israeli Defence Force (IDF) had gained considerable ground, Prime Minister Menachem Begin was then forced to modify his fierce demands when faced with threats of Soviet intervention to aid Syria, as well as American disapproval of the invasion.

The IDF's siege of Beirut culminated in some 7000 PLO fighters abandoning the city and fleeing Lebanon into sympathetic Arab sanctuaries in Syria, Jordan, Sudan, North and South Yemen, Algeria, Iraq and Tunisia, where their leader Yasser Arafat set up his headquaters.

On 28 September President Reagan announced that the US Marine Corps was to resume its peacekeeping role in Beirut, which had been interrupted by the Israeli invasion of Lebanon. The Reagan administration stated that it was important that the US maintain a military presence in the area until the Lebanese government was in full control. France, Italy and the United Kingdom also despatched contingents of troops to the region in an attempt to add world pressure to the policing of the area. However, the departure of the PLO ultimately heralded the beginning of a new era of terrorism in Lebanon.

On 18 April 1983, a suicide bomber from Islamic Jihad (a pro-Iranian network of fanatical Shi'ites) drove a truck loaded with 300 lbs of explosives up to the entrance of the US Embassy in Beirut and detonated its deadly cargo, killing 40 people, including eight Americans. A second suicide attack by Hezbollah, again involving a truck packed with explosives (this time some 12,000 lbs of TNT), followed on 23 October. Its target was a four-storey barracks block where more than 300 Marines were billeted. The resulting explosion killed 220 of them, as well as 18 sailors from the US Navy and three US Army soldiers. A simultaneous attack on French paratroopers left 58 dead. A third raid 12 days later claimed the lives of 39 Israeli troops within their guarded camp.

By early 1984 the peacekeeping positions had become untenable and the troops were withdrawn, leaving behind only the Syrians and the Israelis. By February, Lebanon was once again embroiled in an ever-worsening civil war.

The resurgence of Islamic Fundamentalism in the region had been sparked off by the rise to power of the Ayatollah Khomeini in Iran on 1 April 1979, when he declared the country to be an Islamic Republic. Khomeini was a zealot whose unquestioned devotion to Islam was only equalled by his all-consuming hatred for the West and, in particular, the United States. According to most Western intelligence sources, Islamic Fundamentalism was the most destabilising influence in the Middle East throughout the 1980s.

Once again, the capabilities of the SR-71 would be called upon in this hot spot to serve the needs of the transatlantic intelligence community, and of those friendly nations who also shared in the revelations of the 'Habu's' high quality photographic and electronic surveillance. Missions over Lebanon were flown by Det 4 crews in order to keep tabs on the Syrian and Israeli armies, as well as on the supply of contraband to Islamic Jihad warriors and other supporting groups. These flights also monitored the movements of key terrorist leaders in their small executive aircraft, which slipped from one tiny airstrip to another in the region.

One such Middle Eastern SR-71 sortie took place on 27 July 1984, when, at 0730 hrs, Majs 'Stormy' Boudreaux and Ted Ross departed Mildenhall in 64-17979 using the call sign 'Boyce 64'. This important flight (the crew's 30th together) was complicated by several factors – the usual refusal of overflight transit across France, which necessitated entering the Mediterranean area via the Straits of Gibraltar; inlet control problems during acceleration to high Mach, which forced Boudreaux to 'go manual' on bypass door operations; and spike control problems at Mach 2.2, which made the aircraft difficult to fly accurately.

By this time 64-17979 was heading eastbound and nearing Mach 2.5, and its flightpath saw the aircraft committed to entering the Mediterranean on a preplanned course, or overflying West Africa or Spain during an abort. Consequently, Boudreaux elected to 'go manual' on both inlet spike and door operations. Emergency operating procedures dictated that an aircraft in a 'double-manual' configuration should

The nose section and fuselage fore-body chine provided housing for the SR-71's varied reconnaissance gathering equipment (*Lockheed*)

64-17979 launches from Mildenhall on yet another sortie during *Eldorado Canyon* – note the two C-130s in 'Europe One' camouflage parked in the background. (*Paul F Crickmore*)

As with all operations undertaken by Det 4 throughout the 1980s, the unit relied heavily on tanker support during *Eldorado Canyon* (*Lockheed*)

not be flown above Mach 3 and 70,000 ft. Boudreaux, therefore, held the jet at the degraded limit and pressed on through the Straits of Gibraltar high over the Mediterranean. Off the southern coast of Italy, the crew decelerated and descended for a second refuelling.

Standard procedures (once they had returned to subsonic flight) included resetting all inlet switches back to 'automatic', and to continue the next leg of the flight in 'auto', since such inlet 'glitches' often tended to clear themselves on another acceleration cycle. The crew followed this logical procedure, but 64-17979 repeated the previous disturbances. At that point, 'according to the book', they should have aborted the flight. The mission had been planned around a single high-speed, high-altitude pass over the target area. The well-seasoned crew reasoned that they had already come so far that they could easily make that one pass and collect the needed reconnaissance data within imposed operating constraints, especially since they could 'break off' over the waters of the eastern Mediterranean should they have any serious difficulties over land.

Consequently, they completed the reconnaissance run 'manually', but then found that 64-17979 (operated in the less fuel-efficient 'manual' inlet configuration) had ended the run in a notably depleted fuel state. Ross urgently contacted the tankers, which were orbiting near the island of Crete and asked that they head east to meet the thirsty 'Habu'. As the

SR-71 descended, Boudreaux caught sight of the tankers some 30,000 ft below him, and executed what he described loosely as 'an extremely large variation of a barrel-roll', slidding in behind a KC-135Q 'in no time flat'. The boomer plugged in immediately, and 64-17979 began taking on the much-needed JP-7. Hooking up well east of the normal ARCP, 'Boyce 64' had to stay with the tankers much longer than the usual 12 to 15 minutes 'on the boom' in order to drop off at the scheduled end-ARCP, before proceeding back to England.

With the SR-71's tanks filled to a pressure disconnect, Boudreaux and Ross climbed to high altitude on the final leg back through the Straits of Gibraltar and headed home to Mildenhall, where they landed after nearly seven hours – four of which had been spent at supersonic speed while manually controlling both inlet spikes and doors.

The good news was that their 'take' was of exceptional quality as a result of a cold front that covered the eastern Mediterranean and produced very clear air for 'razor sharp' photographic imagery. Det 4's commander, Col Jay Murphy, was especially proud of his crew's very notable mission accomplishments. The bad news was that they had flown a 'degraded' aircraft within range of a known Soviet SA-5 SAM site. Overweighing that concern, however, was word from Washington, DC that the 'take' was 'most valuable' for the analysts back at the National Photographic Interpretation Center (NPIC).

LIBYA

On 1 September 1969, a group of revolutionary army officers seized power while King Idris of Libya was on holiday in Turkey. In a revolt led by a subaltern named Moamar Ghadaffi, the officers proclaimed Libya to be a republic in the name of 'freedom, socialism and unity'. The US government recognised the new regime just five days later, allowing Ghadaffi to consolidate his position of power over the next two-and-a-half years. He nationalised foreign banking and petroleum interests within Libya, and was called a 'strongman' by Western news editors.

Ghadaffi soon made his interpretation of 'freedom, socialism and unity' clear to the world on 11 June 1972 when he announced he was giving aid to the Irish Republican Army. That support was also extended to similar terrorist organisations within Europe and the Middle East.

In the summer of 1981, Ghadaffi decided to lay claim to territorial rights over much of the Gulf of Sidra off Libya's northern coastline. The United States government refused to recognise any extension beyond the traditional three-mile limit, and to back up its 'international waters' claim to the gulf, the aircraft carrier USS *Nimitz* (CVN-68), attached to the Sixth Fleet, began a missile firing exercise within the disputed area on 18 August. Interference by Libyan Mirage IIIs, Su-22s, MiG-23s and MiG-25s culminated in the shooting down of two Su-22 'Fitter-Js' by F-14A Tomcats from VF-41 'Black Aces'. Libyan-American relations plummeted to an all time low as Ghadaffi's aggression continued.

Over the next few years, neighbouring northern Chad was annexed by Libyan forces, an English police woman was shot dead by a Libyan 'diplomat' in London, arms were sent to Nicaraguan Sandinistas and continued support was given to terrorist organisations throughout the world.

By July 1985 US patience was running out, and in an address to the American Bar Association on the 8th of that month, President Reagan branded Libya, Iran, North Korea, Cuba and Nicaragua as members of a 'confederation of terrorist states'. Libya's political ruse finally reached its end after further actions in the Gulf of Sidra, the hijacking of a TWA Boeing 727 airliner on a flight from Rome to Athens and the bombing of the *La Belle* discotheque in Berlin. The latter event on 5 April 1986, which killed two US servicemen and a Turkish civilian, was the catalyst that finally prompted the Reagan administration into action.

However, Det 4 had been planning for a potential strike on Libyan targets since late 1985, as RSO Maj Frank Stampf recalled;

'The week before Christmas, while enjoying the holiday company of a group of friends, their wives and significant others at an evening cocktail party, my pager started to buzz. I had to fight off the urge to make believe I hadn't noticed it. I was finally beginning to relax and get into the holiday spirit, and now it appeared I was to be slapped back into reality by a call from "Mother SAC". I excused myself and called the SRC operations desk to see what was up. I was hoping it was just a routine notification of a sortie delayed or cancelled for weather somewhere very, very far away. No such luck. I was told by the duty officer that I was needed at SAC HQ immediately, and that I should bypass the SRC and go directly to the tanker shop downstairs in the bowels of the building. I made my apologies to the hosts, and very reluctantly left the warm glow of the party for the cold, wet, snowy December streets of Omaha.

'Driving toward the base, I was perplexed as to the reason for my "recall". Not that I hadn't been called in at all odd hours many times before in the almost three years I had been chief of the SR-71 branch at SRC. It was just that normally the duty officer could give me a hint as to the reason. For example, just the word "delay" or "cancel" or "weather" would be enough to give me the general idea of what was going on (without compromising classified information about specific missions, locations, times, etc.) so that I could begin to formulate possible options on my way to the base. Not this time. And being told to report to the tanker operations shop, rather than the SRC, was another surprise.

Maj Frank Stampf (right) headed the SR-71 SRC at SAC HQ in Omaha, Nebraska, during *Eldorado Canyon*. He is seen here as a captain with his pilot, Capt Gil Bertelson. As a crew, they were involved in the important missions that monitored political unrest in Poland during the late winter of 1981 (*Frank Stampf*)

'Of course, we worked with the tanker guys all the time – their support was critical to the success of the SR mission. In fact, aerial refuelling support for all kinds of fighter, bomber, reconnaissance and mission support operations worldwide was coordinated and tasked through the tanker shop at SRC. They had the "big picture" when it came to tanker availability and capabilities.

'As I walked into the tanker vault (pretty much all of the operations areas in the HQ SAC building were in secure "walk-in vaults", where classified information could

73

be openly displayed and readily handled by authorised personnel), I recognised most of the people standing around as tanker guys, some folks from the airborne command and control division, and a bunch of intelligence types. Almost all were in civilian clothes, as I was, since they had also been called in unexpectedly from what they thought would be a quiet evening with friends or family.

'After a few more minutes, when someone decided that everyone who needed to be there had arrived, we were quietened down and the colonel who ran the tanker ops division stood up. He told us that SAC had just received orders from the Pentagon to develop plans for tanker and reconnaissance support for a bombing raid on Libya. The targets were to be terrorist training compounds and military facilities such as airfields, air defences, command and control centres, etc. The raid would take place before dawn, and be immediately followed (at first light) by an SR-71 overflight of the target areas to assess bomb damage, which would be critical in determining whether follow-on strikes would be necessary. My first thought was that the timing for the SR-71 overflight would put the jet overhead just when the Libyans were fully alerted, and very pissed off.

'Apparently, President Reagan had finally decided that he had had just about enough of Moamar Ghadaffi. The US response was to be called Operation *Eldorado Canyon*. The specific date for the attack was not given, but we were to begin planning our respective roles immediately, and have enough information assembled to provide a briefing to the SAC Deputy Commander for Operations and Director of Intelligence (both two-star generals) by 0700 hrs the next day – just ten hours from our initial notification. It was going to be the first of many long nights.

'We obviously wouldn't have the whole operation nailed down in great detail by then, but we were to be prepared to present the various courses of action and recommendations to the SAC General Staff. Then the rest of our resources would be called in and we would begin in earnest to put together the many pieces of what would turn out to be a pretty complex operation.

'The actual attacks would be carried out by US Navy fighter-bombers operating from a carrier in the Mediterranean and USAFE F-111Fs flying out of RAF Lakenheath. They would be supported by RAF Upper Heyford-based USAFE EF-111s (electronic jamming aircraft), a number of command and control aircraft and, of course, about a "bazillion" tankers.

An F-111F from the 494th TFS/48th TFW drops parachute-retarded 500-lb bombs over a range in Spain during a training mission in the late 1980s (*USAF*)

The weather conditions faced by Det 4 crews were guaranteed to be varied compared to those back at Beale. Here, 64-17964, call sign 'Sheik 99', launches from a snow-covered runway in February 1987 (*Paul F Crickmore*)

'Obviously, the US Navy and USAFE fighter-bomber community did the planning for their attack aircraft. The F-111 planners passed on their fuel load and mission timing requirements to SAC, and the SAC tanker crowd figured out how many and what types of tankers would be needed, where they could locate the tracks to safely (both militarily and politically) conduct air refuelling operations, where the tankers would operate from and how and when to get them where they needed to be.

'This was never going to be an easy task, although it started out significantly less complex than it ended up. The original concept for the USAFE strike component called for eight primary F-111s actually on target, with another four "air spare" aircraft launching and flying to a go/no go point, where they would be told whether they were needed or not (based upon the status of the primary jets). The "operators" – the folks who knew the aircraft and mission capabilities first-hand, and who were best qualified to make the call – seemed pretty satisfied that those numbers would do the trick.

'However, because the specific date for the attack had not yet been set (or at least it had not yet been shared with us planning the missions), there must have been sufficient time for more and more general officers to get involved in the game. The plan went through several ever-increasingly complex evolutions until the final strike package of USAFE F-111s eventually reached 18 aircraft, with six air spares. This of course exponentially increased the number of tanker aircraft required to get the "armada" of aeroplanes from the UK to Libya and hopefully back again.

'To make matters worse, several weeks into the process the planners were told that the French would not allow any US aircraft, strike or support, to overfly their landmass either on the way to or returning from the strike. All of the aeroplanes would have to fly south, just off the western coast of France, then turn east and thread their way through the Straits of Gibraltar to get over the Mediterranean Sea. That translated into several more hours of flying time for all the aircraft, which in turn would require even more tankers than before.

'Eventually, the plan called for more than 20 KC-135 and KC-10 tanker aircraft to support the USAF strike force, not to mention the SR-71 primary and air-spare aircraft. This was *not* going to be a "low profile" operation. In fact, one of the most serious concerns was how to avoid mid-air collisions between the dozens of aeroplanes that would be traversing the extremely narrow gap of the Straits of Gibraltar in both directions within a short span of time, while radio-silent and without being under air traffic control.

'Fortunately for us "recce types", that planning problem was one of many logistical and operational challenges left to the tanker troops to resolve. All we had to do was put together a plan to get an SR-71 over all the targets on time, with cameras and electronic sensors blazing, defeat what we expected would be very alert and active Libyan defences and then get the jet back to RAF Mildenhall. There, the mission "take" would be processed and the intelligence immediately disseminated to all the people who would be anxiously awaiting the strike results. Among those people were numerous military and civilian "high rollers", including the Chairman of the Joint Chiefs of Staff and the President of the United States, who wanted to be personally assured that the job had been done.

'Normally, "non-routine" SR-71 missions such as this one would have been developed by the planners at the operational detachment from which the sortie was to be flown, and the plan would then be passed back to our people at the SR-71 branch of the SRC for review and approval. This made sense, since the folks at the Dets were the ones who had firsthand knowledge of the operational environment in which the mission would be flown. However, in this case, there were way too many operational, logistical and political variables that were changing on an almost daily basis (and too many senior officers continuing to get involved) for the Det 4 mission planners to keep abreast of developments by themselves.

'Fortunately, in addition to the very capable and experienced planners at the detachments, we had a couple of pretty solid folks working the task at SRC, including one Maj Chuck Holte. Although Chuck was not a former SR-71 crewmember, he had extensive operational experience as an Electronic Warfare Officer, having flown many real-world reconnaissance missions in the RC-135. He was assigned to the SR-71 branch because of his in-depth knowledge of the ever-changing electronic threat environment, and his expertise was most welcome both in the specific planning of "Habu" missions and in the overall development of strategic plans for future defensive systems that would be needed to allow the SR-71 to remain operationally viable.

'Chuck's quiet, efficient manner and subtle sense of humour made him highly respected and very well liked and trusted by all the SR-71 people who knew him, both at headquarters and at the operational sites. As a result, the Det 4 planners at RAF Mildenhall, from where this mission would be flown, welcomed his input in the planning process for this complex, highly visible tasking.

'As the weeks and months went on and the Omaha winter gave way to spring, we still hadn't received a specific date for the attack. Nevertheless, every general in the HQ building wanted daily updates on the plan. The latter, as initially envisioned, would have been ready to go months earlier, but it seemed as though every general officer to whom it was briefed wanted another change or tweak, so it became the proverbial "perpetual motion machine". Consequently, most of us involved in planning the mission had worked every day and some nights, without a break, from the first night we were called out pre-Christmas. That pattern was to continue right up to the day of the attack in April, and for several weeks following, due to the same general officers wanting "after-action" reports and "lessons learned" briefings.

'Chuck's patient nature allowed him to do a remarkable job keeping up with all the changes for the SR-71 mission plan, and coordinating them with the Det 4 folks as they came up. Then one day in mid-spring, almost four months after we'd been given the order to develop the plan for the mission, the morning news headlines told of a terrorist bombing at the *La Belle* discotheque in Berlin. A number of people had been killed and injured, among them American soldiers. Almost immediately, links were reported between the terrorist bombers and Libya. We had the feeling that this incident would be the trigger for the President to give the go-ahead for the strike. We were right. The date for the attack was set for 15 April 1986, and the SR-71 plan was ready.

'At Det 4 – the "pointy end of the spear" – the HABU crews and all their ops support, maintenance, intelligence and tanker support people were well prepared and waiting to go.

'About 48 hours prior to the scheduled SR-71 launch from Mildenhall, the CINCSAC's executive officer called down to SRC and said that the general wanted my boss and me to come up to his office and brief him on the SR element of the mission. I dutifully folded up the mission charts, packed them into our secure brief case and the colonel and I weaved our way through the lower vaults of the headquarters building where we went about our classified work every day (and many nights). We eventually came to the stairs that took us up the several flights to where the sunlight and air were and, not surprisingly, the generals' offices. I'm not sure how many general officers were assigned to SAC headquarters at the time, but I think it would have been easier to count the stars in the Milky Way than the collective stars on their shoulders.

'We made our way to the CINCSAC's office and waited outside under the watchful eye of his trusty exec until the general was ready to receive us. As one of the SAC operations briefers, I had stood in front of the CINCSAC quite a few times before while presenting the daily SAC operations briefing, with my emphasis being placed on the results of all the worldwide reconnaissance missions that had been flown during the previous 24 hours.

'As a frame of reference for this briefing, it was no secret that SAC did not like having the SR-71 within its operating budget. As I was also responsible for articulating and advocating the SR-71 operating budget within SAC, I was constantly locked in a state of mortal combat within the command to increase, or at times just sustain, funding for the flying hours we needed to meet our growing tasking. The problem was that the majority of that tasking was coming from many sources *outside* SAC, and even outside the USAF. For example, the driving reason we established a permanent SR-71 det in Europe was to meet the US Navy's critical need to monitor the status of the Soviet Northern Fleet, and in particular their nuclear submarine operations out of Murmansk, on the Barents Sea.

'Once permanent SR-71 operations were set up and operating in Europe, the US Army realised that we could provide excellent coverage of the Eastern Bloc countries around the Federal Republic of Germany, particularly during the darkness and cloud-covered weather of the European winter. The US Army was also the primary driver of the regular coverage that we provided which allowed it to monitor the North Korean force status and movement in and around the Korean Peninsula.

SAC was not too happy about having to pick up the tab as the benevolent provider of all that great intelligence to other commands and services, especially when it felt that it cut into funding for strategic bombers, intercontinental ballistic missiles and tankers. So it was no surprise that the CINCSAC was not a huge supporter of the SR-71 programme – other than, of course, when SAC wanted to make a splash at airshows or other exhibitions, where the SR-71 was always its star performer and biggest crowd pleaser.

During the May 1986 Mildenhall air fete, 64-17980's performance was accidentally enhanced when, during the course of a knife-edge pass, a build-up of unburned fuel in the engines suddenly ignited with spectacular results. Also of note is the flow pattern of the wing vortices. The previous month, this aircraft had played a key role in obtaining BDA photos of *Eldorado Canyon* targets (*Bob Archer*)

A close-up of the nose of 64-17980 following its return to Beale from Mildenhall in October 1986 (*Lockheed*)

'The general had us lay out the chart with the SR-71 track on his desk, and we were to brief him straight from the map. I had gotten about as far as "Sir, this is . . ." when he jabbed his finger at the two large rings representing the coverage of the Soviet-made SA-5 SAM sites, both of which were clearly bisected by the SR-71's planned track. One was located at Sirt, near the first target area at Benina airfield in eastern Libya, and the other at Tripoli, to the west. The CINC then asked, while continuing to stare at the very large circles on the map, "Will these SA-5s be taken out prior to the SR-71 going in?" My response, I thought at the time, was pretty obvious, even for a lowly major like me. "Sir, we'll know if the sites were destroyed when the SR returns and the intel folks analyse the take". Wrong answer. The remainder of the "briefing" went *something* like this;

'The general – "I don't want the aeroplane penetrating those SAMs unless we know they've been neutralised prior to the pass."

'The lowly major – "Sir, there is no way for the SR to collect all of the tasked targets without going through the SA-5 coverage. The SR will be at better than Mach 3 and at, or above, 80,000 ft. The best intel we have on the SA-5 and the SR's ability to defeat it with the aeroplane's combination of onboard systems, speed and altitude puts this at an acceptable risk level for the mission."

'The general – "Like I said, major, I don't want the SR to penetrate those rings unless we know the sites have been taken out."

The lowly major – "Sir, if we could just . . ."

The general, this time in a clearly angered tone – "Major, you are not *listening*. I'm not going to risk one of *MY* SR-71s for this piddly little operation!"

'The lowly major, in thought only – "One of '*his*' SR-71s? Piddly little operation?"

'End of discussion, end of briefing. Back to the drawing board, and with less than 48 hours to come up with an alternative approach.

'Although the SA-5 was the most modern, and only existing Soviet SAM system with a postulated capability against the SR-71, none had yet been fired at the "Habu", and therefore its capability against a high-altitude, Mach 3+ manoeuvring target was still hypothetical. Additionally, we had more than reasonable confidence in the SR-71's onboard electronic defensive systems, when coupled with the aeroplane's speed and altitude, to handle the threat. On top of all that, this was the very type of mission for which the SR-71 had been designed, and had proven itself so well in successfully accomplishing for over 20 years up to that point. In fact, even when the programme was eventually terminated four years later, the SR-71 boasted a record that no other USAF aircraft could claim. After 26 years of operational service and hundreds of missions over and around hostile territory, with hundreds of SA-2 SAM firings against it during the Vietnam War alone, not a single USAF crewmember had ever been killed in an SR-71 due to enemy action.

'Notwithstanding the reality of all that, we were clearly going to have to come up with another approach if we were going to meet the tasking that had been levied on us. In hindsight, if we had failed to come up with a workable plan, this would have been a perfect way for SAC to say that the SR-71 was tasked, but couldn't support the mission – another arrow in its quiver to get rid of the programme.

'After a lot of scurrying and many secure phone calls, we were told by our people in Washington, DC that there was a *slight* possibility the status of the SA-5 sites could be assessed by a highly classified intelligence source in the short period between the time that the last bomb was dropped and the SR-71 came over the target. So we came up with another plan that none of us liked very much.

'The status of the SAM sites, if known by then, could be transmitted via satellite communications to the KC-10 tanker that would be waiting for the SR-71 over the Mediterranean Sea prior to the latter accelerating into the target area. Once the SR-71 was on the tanker's boom and taking fuel, its crew would simply pass the words "Option Alpha" or "Option Bravo" to the SR crew via the secure boom interphone. The SR-71 RSO would then select one of two flightpaths pre-programmed into the ANS computer. From the end of the air refuelling track, "Option A" would direct the aeroplane along the originally planned flightpath directly through the SA-5 rings, assuming that intel had confirmed that the sites had been destroyed.

'If the sites were either confirmed as still operational, or the information simply wasn't available, then the RSO would select "Option B", which would take the SR on a peripheral flightpath that skirted the operational range of the SA-5s. This flightpath would obviously allow the SR-71 to avoid the potential SA-5 threat, but it would also reduce the number of targets its sensors could collect, and therefore degrade the usefulness of the intelligence it would bring back.

'We at SRC didn't like this plan for any number of reasons. First of all, *no* SR-71 crew liked to mess around with the ANS once the jet was airborne and operating

This was the map used by Pentagon officials to brief the media on the route taken by USAF strike packages from Lakenheath and Upper Heyford to Libya during *Eldorado Canyon* (*DoD*)

smoothly. The system was certainly capable of doing what was planned in this case, but it just didn't *"feel"* right to the crews. But more importantly, by not allowing the SR-71 to fly the mission as originally planned to acquire *all* the tasked damage assessment of the targets hit by the strike force, there was a great risk of not knowing what was and what wasn't destroyed. This would very likely result in sending more aircraft in for a second strike. As it was, we lost one F-111F crew in the first attack. Another strike, especially if launched unnecessarily – only because the SR-71 wasn't *allowed* to confirm which targets had already been hit – would just expose more aircrews to the danger of losing their lives for no reason.

'But, as ordered, we passed the revised "Option A/B" plan to the Det planners, and they prepared to execute it as the SR-71's launch time approached. Frustration levels were high all around. This was one of those times when the crews on the line, getting ready to fly the mission, no doubt wondered what in the world was going on in the minds of their former crewmates at the headquarters who had tasked this crazy sortie.

'Ultimately, the "Option A/B" plan was scrapped for some reason undisclosed to us pretty much at the last hour. The SR-71 crew wound up flying the mission as originally tasked, and obviously survived the SA-5 threat to come back with the "take". This came as no surprise to those of us who knew and understood the "Habu", and its incredible capabilities. It is not unreasonable to speculate that the "highly classified source" that was supposed to provide the status of the SAM sites prior to the SR going in wasn't up to the task, and the SAC general staff was beginning to feel the pressure, both from the Joint Chiefs of Staff and from the White House, to produce the much-needed intelligence.'

DET 4 COMMANDER

Lt Col Barry MacKean was the Det 4 commander during this period, and it was up to him and his team to implement the plan, as he recalled for this volume;

'Planning for the raids on Libya in April 1986 began weeks before the actual flights. Maj Frank Stampf from the SRC at HQ SAC in Omaha, Nebraska, initially advised me of the pending operation, codenamed *Eldorado Canyon*. At that point everything was handled as Top Secret because of the implications of overflying foreign territory. There was also a great deal of uncertainty about whether the missions would ever be flown due to the necessary approvals required from several foreign countries – most notably the British government.

'USAF involvement in the plan was to be exclusively executed from England. The F-111F strike would launch from RAF Lakenheath, the EF-111 Raven electronic support aircraft from RAF Upper Heyford, KC-135 and KC-10 refuelling support from RAF Fairford and RAF Mildenhall, while SR-71 reconnaissance support would be fielded from the latter base. Given the enormity of the plan, world sensitivities at the time and the lack of British involvement, I had my doubts that Prime Minister Margaret Thatcher would approve air strikes flown from England. Fortunately for the free world, and in spite of mounting opposition from within her own party, as well as from the Labour Party, she ultimately approved the missions.

TARABULUS
AZIZIYAH BKS
SIDI BILAL
TRIPOLI
MILITARY AIRPORT
BENGHAZI
JAMAHIRIYAH BKS ▲▲ BENINA AIRBASE
FIR

Pentagon officials also revealed this map to the press when detailing the targets attacked during *El Dorado Canyon* (*DoD*)

Three EF-111 Ravens from the 42nd Electronic Countermeasures Squadron accompanied the F-111Fs during the *Eldorado Canyon* strikes, jamming Libyan radars (*USAF*)

'The SR-71 mission was to provide BDA for all the target areas struck in Libya. US Navy strike aircraft were targeting Benghazi, in the eastern part of Libya, while the USAF was attacking military installations in Tripoli and surrounding areas. An additional burden was placed on all Air Force sorties to fly around France, Spain and Portugal, then through the Straits of Gibraltar, because the French government refused to grant the USAF overfight clearance.

'The sensor chosen by the Pentagon for the "Habu" mission was a suite of highly sensitive cameras. This choice was based on the ability of intel personnel to declassify the photo images for release to the world's press, whereas products generated from our HRR system would reveal their capabilities and, therefore, could not be declassified. This decision would prove operationally restrictive for us, however, as although the radar was day/night all-weather capable, the wet film cameras were restricted to daytime missions in clear weather only.

'Our mission planning team, led by Maj Bruce Blakely under the supervision of the Director of Operations Lt Col Bob Behler, developed a very creative flight profile for the SR-71 that maximised target collection while minimising exposure to SAMs and Libyan fighters. Since we had previously flown missions into the eastern Mediterranean area, the same aerial refuelling track was selected to help disguise this mission. It consisted of a high altitude route that unexpectedly turned back to the west, covering the targets in eastern Libya, before proceeding at Mach 3+ to the capital, Tripoli. The speed at which these photo passes were flown would give the Libyan air defence systems little time to respond.

'When it appeared that *Eldorado Canyon* "might" be approved, the build up of tanker aircraft, both KC-10s and KC-135s, began at RAF Mildenhall. Part of the cover story for this highly visible addition of tankers parked everywhere on base was that a large European exercise, normally scheduled for this time of year, was taking place. There were even photographs and stories in local British newspapers to that effect, which helped minimise any potential leaks.

'To add further credence to this ruse, and disguise the real operation, at 0500 hrs on the morning of the actual mission (the strike aircraft and tankers launched from UK bases at around 1700 hrs later that same day) the 48th Tactical Fighter Wing at RAF Lakenheath initiated a typical base "exercise". This included a recall of all military personnel to their duty stations, generation of aircraft for alert, including uploading conventional weapons, and the instigation of general exercise activities. Many of the "exercise" participants were completely unaware of what was about to happen later that day.

'Launch of the strike force and tankers occurred in the late afternoon on Monday, 14 April. The day prior, I had received a call from Maj Stampf at SRC directing us to cancel our regularly scheduled sorties and configure both of our jets for the pending Libyan mission. One aircraft was designated as primary, with the other scheduled to follow a little over an hour later as back-up in case the primary SR-71 had to abort for mechanical or sensor problems.

'Our maintenance team, led by Mel Rushing, consisted of 45 Lockheed personnel, with 15 subcontractors and associates from other companies that supported systems/sensors on the aircraft. I had two "blue-suit" (USAF) technical sergeants (Robby Butterfield and Jerry Gresham) that provided me with quality assurance of the contractor maintenance. The intelligence branch consisted of about 100 military personnel led by Maj Rod Mitchell. This team provided the targeting data for mission planning, processed the film after the mission, analysed the imagery for weapons' effects and managed all the electrical and conditioned air requirements for the American systems operating under British standards. Bottom line, the entire team was extremely anxious to participate in Operation *Eldorado Canyon*.

'Our scheduled launch time was 0500 hrs on Tuesday, 15 April. It was hoped that by the time the jet reached Libya there would be enough light in the target areas to effectively expose the camera film and reveal the damage. With our aircraft and team in full readiness, I departed my office at around 1700 hrs on 14 April for my on-base quarters at RAF Lakenheath. My staff car was equipped with UHF/VHF radios that allowed me to monitor our operation, as well as that of the tower at RAF Mildenhall. The most amazing thing was happening on the taxiways and runway – tankers were taxiing and taking off without communicating with the tower or departure control. The entire operation was performed "comm out" – all movement and approvals were done with lights from the tower based on timing. It was truly an amazing sight to behold!

'As I approached my quarters, I witnessed the same "comm out" launch of the F-111Fs, fully loaded with their conventional stores. My wife Terri, an Air Force nurse stationed at the hospital at RAF Lakenheath, had participated in the early morning exercise/recall that day. When I entered the house she told me how for the first time ever an exercise had been terminated early. The cover story was that the exercise had gone so well that the wing staff chose to terminate the remaining events. I gave her a set of binoculars and told her to look at the next F-111 that took off. She too was amazed to see the conventional weapons on the wings. I then told her about *Eldorado Canyon*.

'After a few hours of restless sleep I returned to our unit to find everything in perfect shape. We launched the primary aircraft, flown by Lt Col Jerry Glasser and RSO Maj Ron Tabor, "on the hack, comm out". After our spare aircraft, flown by Majs Brian Shul and RSO Walt Watson launched successfully, several of us went for breakfast. As we got out of the car, the F-111s were returning one by one back into RAF Lakenheath, but this time there were no weapons on the wings – definitely an eerie sight. Unfortunately, one F-111 had been lost with its crew and another had been forced to land in Spain with engine problems.

'Remember the earlier comment about cameras requiring good weather? Well, we encountered our nemesis – cloud-cover over the target area. The primary aircraft flew perfectly and did everything required, but the target areas remained obscured by clouds. Both aircraft came back "code one", meaning not one maintenance discrepancy. Before we even received word from SRC requesting us to perform a return mission, I had the maintenance teams preparing both aircraft for possible flights the next day. Everyone was so mission oriented there was no problem making it happen. While we awaited the go-ahead from SRC, our intelligence team was pouring over the film with the hope of getting enough usable imagery to complete a full BDA report. Unfortunately, when it came to the area around Tripoli there was none to be had.

'With SRC approval, we swapped the aircrews and jets and flew the very next day. Our mission planners cleverly altered the flight plan to preclude predictability and to minimise potential threats. However, on this occasion the lead aircraft experienced a malfunction of the Optical Bar Camera (OBC). Although the other cameras performed flawlessly, the target areas were obscured by sand storms. Because of the high level of national interest, joining our imagery analysts to review the film was Maj Gen Thomas McInerny, the Third Air Force commander stationed at RAF Mildenhall. He understood that we had no control over Mother Nature, and was very supportive of the efforts of our personnel. However, senior leadership was adamant that we provide releasable BDA.

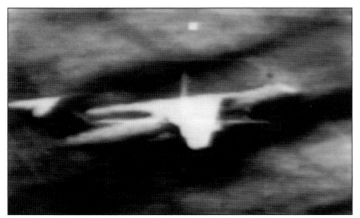

This blurred view of a Libyan air force Il-76 'Candid' transport aircraft parked at Tripoli Airport was taken from footage shot by a 'Pave Tack'/laser-guided bomb delivery system fitted to one of the 48th TFW F-111Fs. The Il-76 was struck by a bomb just seconds after this image was recorded (*USAF*)

'Without missing a beat, our team prepared both aircraft for a third consecutive flight. SRC gave approval and the two jets departed Mildenhall for the third, and finally successful, time. The primary crew consisted of Lt Cols Bernie Smith and RSO Denny Whalen, with the spare crew being Lt Col Jerry Glasser and Maj Ron Tabor. As fate would have it, the target area was clear and we were able to provide good BDA as tasked. However, this was all very frustrating to us in the "recce" team because we knew that we could have provided BDA imagery after the very first sortie had we been allowed to use our very sophisticated radar system.

'Besides finally providing the much sought after BDA, our team established a benchmark for SR-71 sorties generated and flown that was to remain unparalleled. We flew six sorties in three days with only two aircraft supported by a maintenance team that was staffed to support only two to three sorties a week. As the commander of the unit, I was extremely proud of their accomplishments, and the manner in which everyone pulled together. Definitely in keeping with the "Habu" tradition!'

BENINA AIRFIELD
15 APR 86

DESTROYED MIG-23/FLOGGER

MIG-23/FLOGGER PIECES

The results of 64-17980's OBC BDA pass over Benina airfield in the wake of the F-111F strike were released to the world's media, although their source was never officially acknowledged (*USAF*)

MISSION EXECUTION

Lt Col Jerry Glasser, an SR-71 Instructor Pilot and Director of Simulator Training with over 900 hrs of 'Habu' flight time already under his belt, together with his RSO Maj Ron Tabor, an RSO instructor and the chief back-seat simulator instructor, were the primary aircraft crew that would conduct post-strike BDA surveillance after the attack. Majs Brian Shul and his RSO Walt Watson were nominated to fly back-up first time around. A third crew, Lt Col Bernie Smith, the Chief of the Standards Board, and instructor RSO Lt Col Dennie Whalen were en route via a KC-135Q to join their colleagues. They would fly a later mission over Libya. Glasser now provides a unique insight into that first sortie;

'As the tasking came down and the F-111s geared-up, we were directed to equip the aircraft with optical sensors, an OBC in the nose and TEOCs (Technical Objective Cameras) in the chine bays. The weather could always be a problem with visual sensors, but they provided the best image quality, and this was very important for the Reagan administration back in Washington, DC.

'The plan was to launch the two aircraft with a time interval between them which would ensure that if all went according to plan, primary would just be coming off the target as back-up ("air spare") was just about to turn onto the Mediterranean refuelling track. If primary had sustained some kind of mechanical or sensor malfunction, back-up would continue into the area and get the take. If, however, primary cleared the target area and reported "Ops Normal", back-up would turn back for home prior to the Straits of Gibraltar. Three aerial refuelling tracks were planned to support the mission – one off Land's End and two in the Mediterranean. This was due to the French refusing to grant us over-flight permission, which we weren't particularly pleased about, but came as no great surprise to us.

'An area of concern for us as crewmembers was the decision that the second aerial refuelling in the Med was to be conducted from a KC-10 at

Following Det 4's unprecedented operational effort between 15 and 17 April 1986, 64-17980 emerged with mission markings in the form of three red camels applied to the left nose-gear door (*Paul F Crickmore*)

31,000 ft. This was 6000 ft above our usual refuelling block altitude. Checking the Mach/IAS limits for the KC-10 confirmed that we'd be "well behind the subsonic power curve while on the boom". From what I recall, even the KC-10/SR-71 compatibility checks carried out at Palmdale didn't get up to 31,000 ft. A second, and common, problem as we later learned at firsthand was the "brutal sun angle", which would be directly down the boom as we refuelled.

'Mission brief was at 0300 hrs. Brian and Walt were also our mobile crew, so after seeing us off, they had to get suited up and launch as airborne back-up. Our route was subsonic to Land's End, where we'd be topped-off by two KC-135s. We'd then climb and accelerate south along the Portuguese coast, make a left turn through the Straits of Gibraltar, decelerate and refuel in the western Med. Our second acceleration was on an easterly heading, and we'd then make a right climbing turn to the south and head directly for our first target – Benghazi. We'd then perform a hard right to slip by the SA-5 sites at Sirte, before setting course for Tripoli – our second target. The plan then called for a post-target deceleration for our third, and final, aerial refuelling in the western Med,

Lt Col Jerry Glasser and his RSO Maj Ron Tabor secured vital *El Dorado Canyon* BDA intelligence in 64-17980. The same aircraft is seen here ten days after the Libyan strike, the jet still being equipped with its 'glass nose' – the latter housed an Itek Corporation OBC. Imagery taken by the crew of this 'Habu' was released to the world's media (*Bob Archer*)

El Dorado Canyon chalked up many firsts for Det 4, including refuelling from a KC-10 Extender tanker in-theatre (*Lockheed*)

before our final acceleration saw us exit through the Straits onto a northerly heading that would take us back to the UK.'

The main thrust of the strike was to be conducted by 18 F-111Fs from RAF Lakenheath, split into six flights of three aircraft each using call signs 'Puffy', 'Lujan', 'Remit', 'Elton', 'Karma' and 'Jewel'. More than 20 KC-10s and KC-135s were used to provide aerial refuelling support for the strike force. In addition, three EF-111 Ravens were to provided ECM coverage for the strikers.

Hours before the 'Habu' launched, the first of its support tankers got airborne. Four KC-135s and KC-10s left the base for their refuelling orbits, 'Finey 50' (KC-135 59-1520) and 'Finey 51' (KC-10 83-0079) launching at 0230 hrs and 0240 hrs, respectively. 'Finey 52' (KC-135 58-0125 and 'Finey 53' (KC-10 83-0082) launched at 0402 hrs and 0405 hrs, followed by 'Finey 54' (KC-135 60-0342) and 'Finey 55' (KC-135 58-0094) at 0412 hrs and 0415 hrs. Finally, 'Finey 56' (KC-10 83-0075) left Mildenhall at 0740 hrs.

Lt Col Jerry Glasser and Maj Ron Tabor took-off as scheduled at 0500 hrs in SR-71 64-17980 (call sign 'Tromp 30'). Lt Col Glasser continues;

'For take-off we carried 55,000 lbs of fuel, which was 10,000 lbs more than normal. A night launch down Mildenhall's 8500-ft runway was always exciting. From a safety aspect, I always had concerns for the buildings at the end of runway 29, especially when we were heavy. We rendezvoused as planned with "Finey 54" and "Finey 55", which had entered a holding pattern off the southwest coast of England. Our first aerial refuelling was fine except for a little turbulence. We then made our first acceleration towards the Med.

'The early morning acceleration with the sunrise and the coast of Europe to the left painted a wonderful scene, and the turn through the Straits of Gibraltar was quite spectacular – we were prohibited from taking random photos of the Straits, however.

'For our second aerial refuelling, we planned to have a KC-135Q act as lead to a KC-10 in trail. This was because of the special comm/ranging equipment that was unique to our dedicated tankers. We thought the addition of an extra tanker was overkill, but things worked out just fine. The KC-135Q flew one mile ahead of the KC-10 and we ranged on both.

'The weather was clear but the sun angle was a big problem. As we hooked-up at 31,000 ft, I couldn't see the tanker's director lights due to the glare. I'd talked to the KC-10 boomer prior to the mission, and this proved to be an invaluable conversation. As a result of our chat on the ground, he fully understood the speed/altitude incompatibility issue, and that the sun angle was likely to cause a problem. I had two boom disconnects before I settled down, and to further help reduce the glare, Ron got the tanker to turn ten degrees right and I "hid" under its number one engine nacelle. When we reached 53,000 lbs of JP-7 on-load, I put both throttles into min-burner to stay on the boom – normally, we'd engage the left burner at about 77,000 lbs (dependant on the outside air temperature) in order to get a full fuel load from a KC-135 at our usual altitude.

'Ron did a masterful job managing the on-load – he knew I was just hanging on for the last 27,000 lbs to complete a full off-load. Knowing that the director lights were of no help to me, the KC-10 boomer also did a fine job keeping us plugged in. When we'd finally finished, we began our second acceleration. I have to say that I've completed many aerial refuellings in the SR-71 in good and bad weather on pitch black nights, even in an area we called the "black hole" over the Pacific, off Kadena, at night, with no moon and in rough weather. However, that second aerial refuelling was my most challenging ever.

'As we began the second acceleration, the right afterburner wouldn't light, but a little manual rise in exhaust temperature, together with another shot of TEB (TriEthylBorane – JP-7 was so inert that it had to be kindled by use of TEB, which ignited spontaneously on contact with oxygen), and we were off again. We entered a solid cirrus deck at 41,000 ft, and I began to get a little concerned when we didn't break out until we reached 60,000 ft. However, as soon as we were clear, dead ahead of us was the coast of Africa, and Ron got set for the Benghazi take. As we levelled off at 75,000 ft at our cruising speed of Mach 3.15, the jet was running just beautifully. I knew to leave Ron alone during this phase, as he was really busy. The DEF warning lights started to flash and Ron signalled that all was a GO. The take seemed normal as we made our hard right turn towards Tripoli, and we were tuned for the SA-5 site at Sirte. Again, warning lights flashed, but nothing was visible – we truly felt invincible at Mach 3.15.

'The weather over Tripoli wasn't good. As we completed the run and turned out of the area, Ron gave an "OPS NORMAL" call, so Brian and Walt, who were fast approaching the pre-designated abort point, made a right turn short of Gibraltar and headed back to Mildenhall. As it subsequently turned out, morning fog cut out some of the optical take around Tripoli and two more missions would be required to complete the BDA picture – one due to weather and the other because of OBC failure.

'Our third, and final, refuelling, conducted down at 26,000 ft, was uneventful. We pressure disconnected off the boom and headed home once again through the Straits. The remainder of the mission was "normal, normal, normal", as Ron and I made our final descent into the UK and called "London Mil". I still plainly recall the impeccable English of the Air Traffic Controller that gave us both a little lift. "Good morning gentleman. It's been a long day for you". I feel some nostalgia, and a great sense of pride, when I think back to the professional relationship Det 4 had with British controllers.

'As we were handed over to the various controlling agencies on our way back to Mildenhall, we were eventually vectored to runway 11 for a ground-controlled approach. The landing was uneventful, and as we taxied back to the "barn", there was Brian, Walt, Bernie and Dennie in the "mobile car" to greet us. But as was my habit, as I stepped from the gantry ladder, the people I first made sure to shake hands with were the maintenance chiefs who, through their professionalism, had enabled Ron and I to fulfill our part of the mission.'

As planned, Majs Brian Shul and Walt Watson had launched at 0615 hrs in aircraft 64-17960 (call sign 'Tromp 31') and duplicated the route flown by Glasser and Tabor to the first ARCP with 'Finey 54' and '55' off Cornwall. Shul spotted the returning F-111s approaching head-on, several thousand feet below. 'Lujac 21's' pilot (the F-111 flight leader) duly rocked his wings in recognition and Shul returned this time honoured aviation salute with a similar manoeuvre.

The final tanker (KC-10 83-0075) assigned to refuel the F-111s on their return flight during *Eldorado Canyon* was re-rolled 'on the wing' to help out the returning 'Habus' once the strikers had reached Lakenheath.

At 0910 hrs, some four hours after the SR-71s had launched, a KC-135Q (call sign 'Java 90') landed at Mildenhall carrying senior members of the 9th SRW staff from Beale to witness the mission debriefing. Twenty minutes later, tankers 'Finey 54' and

64-17980 deployed to Det 4 on four occasions, and it is seen here being made ready to participate in the static display at the 1987 Mildenhall air fete during its final visit to the UK (*Paul F Crickmore*)

'55' touched down, followed at 0935 hrs by 'Tromp 30', which had flown a mission lasting four-and-a-half hours. One hour and 13 minutes later Shul and Watson landed in the back-up 'Habu', 'Tromp 31'. The five remaining tankers returned over the next four-and-a-half hours, 'Finey 51' having flown a twelve-and-a-half hour sortie. When 'Finey 56' landed at 1526 hrs, *Eldorado Canyon* was completed, with the exception of search efforts for Capts Fernando Ribas-Domminici and Paul Lorence, whose F-111F had been lost the previous night off the coast of Libya.

The mission's 'take' was processed in the MPC and then transported by a KC-135 ('Trout 99') to Andrews AFB, Maryland (only 25 miles from the Pentagon and the White House), where national-level officials were eagerly awaiting post-strike briefings that showed both the good and bad effects of the strike. The world's media had been quick to report the latter aspect of the operation, BBC journalist Kate Adie being used as a propaganda dupe to show not only where one F-111's bomb load had gone astray near the French Embassy, but also where Libyan SAMs had fallen back on the city, only to be labelled as more misdirected US bombs. On a more positive note for the USAF, her reports proved useful in providing post-strike reconnaissance footage of an accurately bombed terrorist camp, referred to by her as an army 'cadet' school.

As mentioned earlier, the marginal weather around the Libyan capital forced another 'Habu' sortie to be flown the following day. This time Jerry Glasser and Ron Tabor were back-up, again in 64-17980, for Brian Shul and Walt Watson, who were the primary crew in 64-17960. Bernie Smith and Dennie Whalen were the mobile crew, charged with overseeing both launches and recoveries back into Mildenhall. However, during this sortie the primary aircraft suffered a sensor failure, and for whatever reason the back-up aircraft, which was in the air and operational, was not notified. This meant that a third mission had to be flown on 17 April, with Smith

On 29 June 1987, during the course of an operational mission into the Baltic to monitor the Soviet nuclear submarine fleet, Majs Duane Noll and Tom Veltri suffered an explosion in the right engine of 64-17964. This photograph was taken by a Swedish air force JA 37 Viggen pilot – note the position of the ejector nozzle on the shutdown engine (*Swedish air force*)

and Whalen as the primary crew in 64-17980, backed-up by Shul and Watson, again in 64-17960.

To preserve security, call signs were changed, with 'Fatty' and 'Lute' being allocated to the tankers and SR-71s, respectively, for the 16 April mission, and 'Minor' and 'Phony' used the next day. Photos taken in the vicinity of Benghazi by 'Tromp 30' on 15 April were released to the press, although the source was never officially admitted and image quality was purposely degraded to hide the system's true capabilities.

Bellicose rumblings from Ghadaffi continued after the raid, and 14 months later, US intelligence services believed that Libya had received MiG-29 'Fulcrums' from the USSR. This outstanding fighter, with a ground attack capability, would considerably enhance Libya's air defence network. It was therefore decided that Det 4 should fly another series of sorties over the region to try and confirm these intelligence reports.

On 27, 28 and 30 August 1987, both SR-71s were launched from Mildenhall to photograph all the Libyan bases. Tanker support for each operation consisted of three KC-135s and two KC-10s. The tankers and the 'Habus' used the call signs 'Mug', 'Sokey' and 'Baffy'. Two other KC-135s ('Gammit 99' and 'Myer 99') flew courier missions to Andrews AFB on 29 August and 9 September to transport the 'take' to the Pentagon, where intelligence analysts failed to find the suspected MiGs .

Thereafter, until 21 December 1988, it appeared as though the Libyan leader and his regime may have learned a lesson about US intolerance towards international terrorism. However, that night, high over the small Scottish town of Lockerbie, Pan American Boeing 747 Flight 103 was blown out of the sky by a bomb that had been planted in luggage loaded onto the aircraft. In all, 259 passengers and crew and at least 11 people on the ground were killed, making this Britain's worst air disaster and terrorist atrocity.

DET 4's NEAR LOSS

Some 18 months earlier, on 29 June 1987, Det 4 had almost suffered an aerial disaster of its own. Majs Duane Noll and RSO Tom Veltri, in 64-17964, were conducting a seemingly routine Barents/Baltic Seas mission when there was an explosion in the aircraft's right engine. Having just

This photo was also taken by the Viggen pilot on 29 June 1987. Note that 64-17964's rudders are clearly angled to the right, pilot Duane Noll having to compensate for the effects of asymmetric thrust from the serviceable left engine (Swedish air force)

Capts Larry Brown (left) and Keith Carter enjoyed the hospitality of the Norwegian air force on 20 October 1987 after they were forced to divert to Bodø following generator failure in 64-17980 (USAF)

Following cancellation of the *Senior Crown* programme, no operational sorties were flown after 30 September 1989 (the end of the USAF's fiscal year). 64-17967, seen here equipped with a panoramic nose section, returns to Mildenhall on 20 November 1989 after completing a functional check flight – its next flight was to be the journey back to Beale (*Bob Archer*)

Maj Tom McCleary (right) and RSO Lt Col Stan Gudmundson bid farewell to the team of Mildenhall-based ground technicians, and the assembled media, before ferrying 64-17964 back to Beale on 18 January 1990 (*Paul F Crickmore*)

Following departure of the first SR-71 from Mildenhall on 18 January 1990, a press conference was held in the Det 4 building. Majs Don Watkins (left) and his RSO Bob Fowlkes were on hand to answer questions, before they in turn ferried 64-17967 back to Beale the next day. Ironically, both men had flown what turned out to be the SR-71's final operational mission from Det 1 at Kadena air base, Okinawa, on 19 September 1989 (*Paul F Crickmore*)

completed their anti-clockwise run off the coasts of Lithuania, Latvia and Estonia, and with 'denied territory' off to their right, the crew had no alternative but to turn left, decelerate and descend. North of Gotland, and with the aircraft descending, Veltri turned on the IFF and declared an emergency on Guard frequency, as he recalls;

'That got the Swedish air force's attention, and a pair of Viggens were on our wing before we reached 18,000 ft. Given that the Soviets were monitoring our activity, I was glad to see a friendly escort. We later found out that the Soviets had launched numerous fighters with orders to force us to land in Soviet territory or shoot us down. The descent from 80,000 ft to 25,000 ft, where the aeroplane began to stabilise, took just a few minutes. The Viggens continued to escort us through the Baltic and along the Polish and East German borders until USAFE F-15s from West Germany intercepted and took over escort duties, but the worst was not yet over.

'Since fuel constraints made it impossible for us to make it back to Mildenhall, we were forced to land at Nordholz Air Base, in West Germany. The engine explosion also caused the complete loss of our auxiliary hydraulic fluids, which

meant no brakes or steering on landing. The base closed off all surrounding roads prior to our arrival inanticipation of our going off the runway. Fortunately for everyone, there was just enough residual hydraulic fluid left in the lines for one application of the brakes. The aeroplane stopped just short of the end of the runway, and that's where we left it for the rest of the day until amaintenance crew from Mildenhall arrived and moved it.'

Four months later, on 20 October, Capts Larry Brown and RSO Keith Carter also experienced an in-flight emergency whilst on a Barents/Baltic Seas mission at night. Flying 64-17980, the crew had completed their reconnaissance runs and were closing on the tanker for their last aerial refuelling when the master warning light came on in the cockpit, telling Brown that the right electrical AC engine-driven generator had disconnected itself from the main AC bus. The ANS also went down at the same time, leaving the RSO without his primary navigation system. Although the second generator in the aircraft continued to function, the crew could not get the right generator back on line, so the aircraft was instructed to land at Bødo.

A short while later the remaining serviceable generator failed, forcing the crew to rely on the emergency AC generator. With diminished cockpit lighting and faltering systems, Brown formated with the KC-135Q and headed for the Norwegian base. Eventually, the stricken SR-71 managed to land at Bødo, where it sat for four days being repaired, prior to being flown back to Mildenhall at subsonic speed.

SHUTDOWN

The end of the Cold War brought with it a stampede to 'cash-in the peace dividend' on the back of promises for a 'new world order'. Twenty years on from such unbridled optimism, and the reality appears somewhat different. For the *Senior Crown* programme, however, the end of the Cold War really was the end of the line. No operational SR-71 flights were flown after 20 September 1989, despite a valiant attempt to resurrect a limited programme in 1995 – this was suspended on 16 April 1996. The bottom line was that the programme had, over the years, lost practically all of its high-powered supporters in SAC, and at a time when funds were tight the SR-71 became an easy target – reconnaissance was always a 'Cinderella' when it came to SAC funding.

Lt Cols Ed Yeilding and J T Vida established a coast-to-coast speed record in 64-17972 on 6 March 1990 when they ferried the aircraft from Palmdale to the National Air and Space Museum at Dulles Airport, in Washington, DC. This aircraft had completed no fewer than six stints at Mildenhall during its time with the 9th SRW (*Lockheed*)

Stacked and ready for transport back to Beale, two SR-71 nose sections are seen in storage at Mildenhall in early 1990. The mission flexibility offered by this feature is readily apparent (*Paul F Crickmore*)

The irony was that the SR-71 provided a vast amount of extremely useful intelligence to many other agencies other than just its parent operator SAC, who had to pick up its operating costs. The *Senior Crown* Programme Element number at the Pentagon was PE 11133F. The first digit (1) denoted the major force programme as strategic – the programme that provides fiscal authority. Had that number been a 3, the programme would have been intelligence funded, which is where the SR-71's budget should have come from all along. That of course could have meant a completely different future for the world's most advanced, jet-powered, aviation programme.

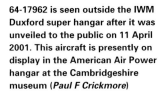

For Det 4, the end came shortly after midday on Friday, 19 January 1990, when SR-71 64-17967, flown by Majs Don Watkins and RSO Bob Fowlkes, departed the runway at Mildenhall for the last time as part of Operation *Busy Relay*. This jet had actually flown Det 4's last recorded sortie (a functional check flight) on 20 November 1989, after which the jets stood idle for almost two months.

The second SR-71 in residence with Det 4 at the time was 64-17964, and it departed for Beale as 'Quid 20', with Majs Tom McCleary and RSO Stan Gudmondson on board, on 18 January 1989. Deactivation of Det 4 took approximately three months, with support equipment being shipped back to the US and reassigned. The 87 military personnel, including Det 4's final CO, Lt Col Tom Henichek, and 76 civilian contractors also returned to Beale.

Some 11 years later, on 4 April 2001, an SR-71 returned to the UK once again when 64-17962 arrived at Tilbury docks from Houston, Texas. It had been in storage at Lockheed Martin's Palmdale facility since its retirement by the USAF on 4 February 1990. Donated to the Imperial War Museum (IWM) for display within its American Air Power hangar at Duxford airfield, in Cambridgeshire, the aircraft had been dismantled by Worldwide Aircraft Recovery and sent by ship to England. Reassembled once on site, 64-17962 was unveiled to the British public on 11 April. To this day, it remains the only SR-71 on display outside the US.

64-17964 rotates from RAF Mildenhall's runway for the last time on 18 January 1990 (*Paul F Crickmore*)

64-17962 is seen outside the IWM Duxford super hangar after it was unveiled to the public on 11 April 2001. This aircraft is presently on display in the American Air Power hangar at the Cambridgeshire museum (*Paul F Crickmore*)

APPENDICES

CHRONOLOGY OF SR-71 DEPLOYMENTS TO THE UK

Aircraft	Deployment Dates
64-17972	9 September 1974 to 13 September 1974
64-17972	20 April 1976 to 30 April 1976
64-17962	6 September 1976 to 18 September 1976
64-17958	7 January 1977 to 17 January 1977
64-17958	16 May 1977 to 31 May 1977
64-17976	24 October 1977 to 16 November 1977
64-17964	24 April 1978 to 12 May 1978
64-17964	16 October 1978 to 2 November 1978
64-17972	12 March 1979 to 28 March 1979
64-17979	17 April 1979 to 2 May 1979
64-17976	18 October 1979 to 13 November 1979
64-17976	9 April 1980 to 9 May 1980
64-17972	13 September 1980 to 2 November 1980
64-17964	12 December 1980 to 7 March 1981
64-17972	6 March 1981 to 5 May 1981
64-17964	16 August 1981 to 6 November 1981 (diverted from Bødo)
64-17958	16 December 1981 to 21 December 1981
64-17980	5 January 1982 to 27 April 1982
64-17974	30 April 1982 to 13 December 1982
64-17972	18 December 1982 to 6 July 1983
64-17971	23 December 1982 to 2 February 1983
64-17980	7 March 1983 to 6 September 1983
64-17955	9 July 1983 to 30 July 1983 (sported false serial '962')
64-17974	2 August 1983 to ? July 1984
64-17958	9 September 1983 to 12 June 1984
64-17979	14 June 1984 to mid-July 1985
64-17975	mid-July 1984 to 16 October 1984
64-17962	19 October 1984 to mid-October 1985
64-17980	19 July 1985 to 29 October 1986
64-17960	29 October 1985 to 29 January 1987
64-17973	1 November 1986 to 22 July 1987 (for repairs)
64-17964	5 February 1987 to mid-March 1988
64-17980	27 July 1987 to 3 October 1988 (from RAF Lakenheath)
64-17971	13 March 1988 to 28 February 1989
64-17964	5 October 1988 (to RAF Lakenheath) to 18 January 1990
64-17967	2 March 1989 to 19 January 1990

COLOUR PLATES

1

SR-71A Article Number 2013 (64-17955), wearing bogus serial 64-17962 of the 9th SRW's Det 4, RAF Mildenhall, 9-30 July 1983

SR-71A 64-17962 first flew on 29 April 1966, and its initial deployment to RAF Mildenhall commenced on 6 September 1976. The jet had previously undertaken two operational deployments to Kadena air base, Okinawa. The aircraft's arrival at Mildenhall on 9 July 1983, therefore, caused little more than the usual level of excitement associated with any SR-71 deployment to the UK. It was a ruse perfectly executed by those within the *Senior Crown* programme that wished to divert close attention away from the aircraft's actual identity. In actuality, a false serial number had been applied to what was in fact SR-71 64-17955 – a platform forever associated with flight test operations at Palmdale. This aircraft was participating in a classified evaluation of a revolutionary ground mapping radar known as the Advanced Synthetic Aperture Radar System. In order to divert unwanted attention away from its duckbill-like nose section that housed the new antenna, groundcrews had relied on artistic

93

deception to mask its true identity, and it worked perfectly – until its radar emissions were monitored by the Soviet Union. The real 64-17962, of course, has resided at IWM Duxford since April 2001.

2

SR-71C Article Number 2000 (64-17981) of the 9th SRW, Beale AFB, March 1969 to April 1976
By any measure SR-71C 64-17981 was a bastard. Its flying characteristics did not measure up to those of the surviving two-seat pilot trainer, 64-17956, and its parentage was frankly very questionable. Following the loss of SR-71B 64-17957 on 11 January 1968, it was deemed necessary to create a hybrid that could substitute for the sole surviving SR-71B whilst the latter was undergoing deep maintenance. Therefore, drastic tri-sonic surgery saw the forebody of a static test specimen mated to the rear section of a retired YF-12A prototype interceptor. Flown for the first time on 14 March 1969, it did a job. Retired in April 1976, the aircraft is presently on display at Hill AFB, Utah.

3

SR-71A Article Number 2006 (64-17955), Air Force Logistics Command, Palmdale, August 1965 to January 1985
SR-71A 64-17955 first flew on 17 August 1965. It was operated exclusively by Air Force Logistics Command from Palmdale, in California, and was the premier SR-71 test bed. Its only known overseas deployment was to RAF Mildenhall from 9 to 30 July 1983 when it tested ASARS whilst marked up as 64-17962. This aircraft made its final flight on 24 January 1985 and was eventually placed on display at Edwards AFB, California.

4

SR-71A Article Number 2027 (64-17976) of the 9th SRW, RAF Mildenhall, 24 October to 16 November 1977
SR-71A 64-17976 flew for the first time in May 1967. It subsequently gained fame by becoming the first 'Habu' to complete an operational mission – an accomplishment achieved on 9 March 1968 over the hostile skies of North Vietnam. The aircraft deployed to RAF Mildenhall on three occasions – 24 October to 16 November 1977, 18 October to 13 November 1979 and 9 April to 9 May 1980. Just prior to the cancellation of the *Senior Crown* programme, a panther was applied (in chalk) to the jet's twin vertical stabilisers. Having accumulated 2985.7 flight hours by the time it was grounded on 27 March 1990, this aircraft is now on display at the USAF Museum at Wright-Patterson AFB, Ohio.

5

SR-71B Article Number 2007 (64-17956), 9th SRW, Beale AFB, 1965 to 1990
One of only two B-models built by Lockheed, this aircraft became the sole survivor after 64-17957 was lost in a non-fatal crash following fuel cavitation while on approach to Beale AFB on 11 January 1968. Pilot operational conversion training onto the 'Habu' was completed via simulator flights and sorties in

the SR-71B. By the time the jet was finally retired by the 9th SRW and NASA, 64-17956 had accumulated no less than 3760 flight hours. It was transferred to the Kalamazoo Air Zoo, in Michigan, and placed on display in December 2002.

6

SR-71A Article Number 2015 (64-17964) of the 9th SRW's Det 4, RAF Mildenhall 16 August to 6 November 1981
SR-71A 64-17964 first flew on 11 May 1966, and by the time it was forced into early retirement in March 1990, the airframe had accumulated 3373.1 flight hours. This jet proved to be a true Anglophile, deploying to RAF Mildenhall on no fewer than six occasions – the highest UK deployment rate of any SR-71. On 12 August 1981, during a scheduled round-robin operational mission from Beale AFB over the Arctic to the Barents/Baltic Seas and back, the aircraft suffered a low oil quality warning in the left engine, forcing its crew to divert to the Norwegian air force base at Bødo. Upon its subsequent positioning flight into RAF Mildenhall, it was seen to be sporting tail-art proclaiming the SR-71 to be *"THE BØDONIAN" EXPRESS*. Clearly enriched by its unscheduled European tour, the aircraft chalked up another unscheduled stop on 29 June 1987 when, following an explosion in its right engine during the course of an operational sortie from Mildenhall into the Barents/Baltic Seas, 64-17964 was forced to shut down its right engine, descend, violate Swedish airspace and divert into Nordholz air base, West Germany.

7

SR-71A Article Number 2010 (64-17959) of Det 51, Palmdale, 20 November 1975 to 24 October 1976
If 64-17981 was 'The Bastard', then 64-17959 fitted with the 'Big Tail' sensor enhancement modification was just plain ugly. First flown on 18 December 1965, it had the new tail fitted a decade later. The latter was almost 9 ft (2.74 m) long, and it was added to increase the SR-71's sensor capacity/ capability. In order to prevent the appendage from contacting the ground during take-off, or being snagged by the brake 'chute during roll out, the tail was hydraulically repositioned eight degrees up or down. The first airborne test was completed on 11 December 1975, and the jet performed the last flight with this unique modification on 24 October 1976. By then it had been decided that such a modification was unnecessary. 64-17959 was permanently grounded five days later and subsequently trucked to the USAF Armament Museum at Eglin AFB, Florida, for permanent display.

8

SR-71A Article Number 2031 (64-17980), 9th SRW, Beale AFB, 1990
SR-71A 64-17980 gained a reputation for being one of the most reliable airframes in the fleet. First flown on 25 September 1967, the aircraft accumulated 2255.6 flight hours before its final sortie with the USAF on 5 February 1990. The jet

undertook its first operational tour from Kadena air base between 12 September 1968 and 19 April 1969. Another Far East deployment followed between 19 June 1971 and 15 August 1972. It first arrived in the UK on 5 January 1982, and returned to Beale three months later. 64-17980 commenced a six-month deployment to Det 4 on 7 March 1983, and a subsequent 15-month detachment began in July 1985. It was during the latter deployment that the jet completed one of its most significant operational missions – a sortie to gather BDA imagery following the raid by USAFE and US Navy strike aircraft on targets in Libya during the early hours of 15 April 1986. 64-17980's fourth, and final, tour in the UK was completed between 27 July 1987 and 3 October 1988.

9
SR-71A Article Number 2031 (64-17980), NASA, Edwards AFB, September 1992 to October 1999
Following cancellation of the *Senior Crown* programme, all SR-71 operational flights around the world ceased on 30 September 1989. Aircraft remaining at Detachments 1 and 4 were eventually returned to Beale, and together with their stable-mates, they were retired from service. Some jets were sent to museums, three were placed in storage at Palmdale and the remaining SR-71B pilot trainer and SR-71As 64-17971 and 64-17980 were loaned to NASA and re-numbered 831, 832 and 844, espectively. On 31 October 1997, the first in a series of experiments began during which 844 flew the Linear Aerospike (LASRE). Three further flights were made before the programme was cancelled in November 1998 after numerous leaks in the LASRE liquid-hydrogen fuel system were detected and it was deemed too expensive to rectify. This aircraft

made the last flight performed by an SR-71 in October 1999, after which it was put on display at NASA's Hugh L Dryden Flight Research Facility at Edwards AFB.

10
SR-71A Article Number 2018 (64-17967) of the 9th SRW's Det 2, Beale AFB, October 1997
First flown on 3 August 1966, 64-17971 made just one deployment to RAF Mildenhall – from 2 March 1989 to 19 January 1990, when its departure to Beale signalled the end of Det 4. Like the rest of the SR-71 fleet, it was retired in 1990. Following intense lobbying over the short-sightedness of prematurely cancelling the *Senior Crown* programme, a 'three-aeroplane SR-71 aircraft contingency reconnaissance capability' was resurrected at a cost of $100 million for Fiscal Year 1995. NASA 831 (SR-71B 64-17956) and 832 (64-17971) were called back to arms, as was this machine, which had been languishing in storage at Palmdale. This programme was eventually cancelled on 10 October 1997 after being line item veto by the then supreme commander of US Forces, President Bill Clinton. Prior to the latter development, Detachment 2 of the 9th SRW had activated at Edwards AFB, and its aircraft adorned with the markings seen on this aircraft. The SR-71's considerable reconnaissance gathering capability had also been further enhanced through the installation of a data-link that allowed digitised ASARS imagery to be transmitted to a ground receiving station in near real-time. All these improvements were ultimately to no avail, however. 64-17967 is presently on display at the Barksdale air force base Museum in Louisiana.

ACKNOWLEDGEMENTS

The material from this volume came from two basic sources – open literature, including books, newspapers, professional journals, various declassified reports and first-hand accounts from pilots, Reconnaissance Systems Officers and other people associated with the various programmes. Much of the information contained within these pages was pieced together during the course of numerous interviews (many of which were taped, others being conducted over the internet) with those intimately connected with the *Senior Crown* programme. Several individuals contributed information with the proviso that their anonymity be respected.

Firstly I owe an immense debt of gratitude to Bob Archer, who went through his vast photographic collection and kindly made available to me some wonderful images that are of significant historical interest to the Det 4 story.

My grateful thanks goes to Cols Don Walbrecht, Frank Murray, Tom Allison, Buddy Brown, Rich Graham, Don Emmons, Ed Payne, Tom Pugh, B C Thomas, Jerry Glasser, Frank Stampf, 'Buzz' Carpenter, Barry MacKean, Curt Osterheld and Rod Dyckman, Lt Cols Blair Bozek and Tom Veltri, Denny Lombard, Thomas Newdick, Dave Adrian, Bob Gilliland, Jim Eastham, Jay Miller, Jeff Richelson, Valery Romanenko, James Gedhardt, Ilya Grinberg, Maj Mikhail Myagkiv, Lutz Freund, Heinz Berger, Rolf Jonsson, Per-Olof Eldh, T D Barnes, Bob Murphy, Paul Eden, Tim Brown, Yefim Gordon and David Allison.

I also wish to thank Maj Gen Pat Halloram, Brig Gens Dennis Sullivan and Buck Adams, Cols Tony Bevacqua, Pat Bledsoe, Larry Boggess, George Bull, Gary Coleman, Ken Collins, Dave Dempster, Bruce Douglass, Carl and Tom Estes, Joe Kinego, Jack Layton, Jay Murphy, Rich Young and Jack Maddison, Lt Cols Nevin Cunningham, Bill Flanagan, Jim Greenwood, Dan House, Tom Henichek, Bruce Leibman, Bob Powell, Maury Rosenberg, Tom Tilden, Ed Yeilding, Reg Blackwell and 'Stormy' Boudreaux, Majs Brian Shul, Doug Soifer and Terry Pappas, and also Keith Beswick, Kent Burns, Russ Daniell, Kevin Gothard, Lindsay Peacock, Betty Sprigg, Rich Stadler, Ellen Bendell and Steve Davies.

Finally, love to my wife Ali, Dad, Neil, Pauline and Nic for their endless support and encouragement.

INDEX